RECEIVING THE
HEALING
GIFT
in MS

*My Journey from Separation to Union after a
Diagnosis of Multiple Sclerosis*

MOUNINA BOUNA ALY

BALBOA.
PRESS
A DIVISION OF HAY HOUSE

Balboa Press books may be ordered through booksellers or by contacting:

Balboa Press
A Division of Hay House
1663 Liberty Drive
Bloomington, IN 47403
www.balboapress.com
1 (877) 407-4847

Because of the dynamic nature of the Internet, any web addresses or links contained in this book may have changed since publication and may no longer be valid. The views expressed in this work are solely those of the author and do not necessarily reflect the views of the publisher, and the publisher hereby disclaims any responsibility for them.

The author of this book does not dispense medical advice or prescribe the use of any technique as a form of treatment for physical, emotional, or medical problems without the advice of a physician, either directly or indirectly. The intent of the author is only to offer information of a general nature to help you in your quest for emotional and spiritual well-being. In the event you use any of the information in this book for yourself, which is your constitutional right, the author and the publisher assume no responsibility for your actions.

Any people depicted in stock imagery provided by Getty Images are models, and such images are being used for illustrative purposes only. Certain stock imagery © Getty Images.

Print information available on the last page.

ISBN: 978-1-5043-9123-8 (sc)
ISBN: 978-1-5043-9124-5 (e)

Balboa Press rev. date: 08/27/2018

I dedicate this book to you who may have received a diagnosis of MS.

I dedicate this book to you who have a loved one who may have received a diagnosis of MS and to anyone helping someone who may have received a diagnosis of MS.

I dedicate this book to you who may be seeking transformation and empowerment.

Contents

Acknowledgments

I have deep gratitude for this miraculous, precious, and mysterious life.

I have deep gratitude for my mother and my father for giving me this precious gift of life. I have deep gratitude for my sister. She is amazing.

I have deep gratitude for Leïla Boukouiss for being my best friend and spiritual sister on this journey of transformation. I have deep gratitude for Hugo Boaknin for having shared this road with me with love.

I have deep gratitude for Francis Bernard. Before he drowned in 2005, he wrote: "Mind over matter." I will remember him and his words always. He was so right. Bless his soul.

I have deep gratitude for the friends I had before this diagnosis of MS.

I have deep gratitude for the beautiful people I have met around the world while I was looking under every rock to find an answer to this puzzling situation.

I have deep gratitude for Marie Lise Labonté. She is a spiritual mother to me. She helped me awaken to the fact that I am a spiritual being—I am a soul. She embodies so beautifully her human dimension and her spiritual dimension.

I have deep gratitude for Sylvie Bérubé who helped me give birth to the feminine side of me. She embodied so beautifully her feminine side and her masculine side. Bless her soul.

I have deep gratitude for Odette Côté and Nathalie Picard for their support during my holistic bodywork training.

I have deep gratitude for Nicolas Bornemisza for his teachings on the unconscious mind. He is such a gentle master.

I have deep gratitude for Dr. Olivier Soulier for his DVD *Sortir de la sclérose en plaques*, which means "coming out of multiple sclerosis," where he explains in depth the meaning of this disease.

I have deep gratitude for the teachings of Dr. Joe Dispenza who helped me demystify the mystical. He introduced me to the concept of changing from the inside out.

I have deep gratitude for the coaching of Mary Morrissey who helped me take a stand and express myself in the world. She is so rigorous, loving, and spiritual.

I have deep gratitude for the written and spoken teachings of Pema Chödrön, Byron Katie, and Eckhart Tolle.

I have deep gratitude for the wisdom of Louise Hay and Dr. Wayne Dyer. Bless their souls.

I have deep gratitude for the genius of Albert Einstein and Carl Gustav Jung. I have deep gratitude for the wisdom of the Buddha and Yogi Bhajan.

I have deep gratitude for my yoga teachers: Yogi Shabad, Pierre Bélisle, and Marie-Daphné Roy.

I have deep gratitude for the amazing massage therapist who I was led to one day: Danielle Tremblay. I have deep gratitude for all the wonderful people I have met on my road to recovery, namely the physiotherapist whom I worked with during my second stay at the Notre-Dame Hospital and the two psychologists I worked with during my two physical rehabilitations.

I have deep gratitude for Mohamed Bouna Aly, Leïla Boukouiss, Teuta Lemghalef, Holley Hood, Fred T. Wyrick, Laura S. Shortridge, and Joy M., my editor from Balboa Press, for their precious help and feedback with my book.

You were all precious guides to me. I thank you all with all my heart, and I love you all!

Foreword

I met Mounina during a training on the body I was offering in the Dominican Republic. She introduced herself as a yoga teacher. During the week, I noticed she had problems with both speaking and walking. Having had in my practice patients suffering from multiple sclerosis, I recognized that Mounina was suffering from this disease, even though she had not informed me.

Then, one morning, she did not show up for the training. I let her rest. When she arrived at the end of the afternoon for the other portion of the training, I decided to ask her about her state. Mounina admitted that she had hidden the fact that she was suffering from this disease. Having healed myself of an autoimmune disease, Mounina came to seek comfort and learning from me.

However, to my astonishment, she was in denial of her disease and had even stopped her medication, thinking that being close to me would heal her. I was greatly surprised by her naivety regarding the healing process. Even though we talked about the importance of medication and acceptance of MS, Mounina was not ready to face her state. There was, at that time, refusal, rebellion, and stubbornness in her.

During the week of the training, Mounina had a severe relapse of her disease. My team and I helped her, brought her to the clinic, and had her sent back to Montreal, Canada. It is through this difficult challenge that I got to know her and recognize her for her courage and determination. Mounina's relapse was due to suddenly stopping her medication. It is through this situation that Mounina gently started changing her attitude.

Afterward, Mounina was always present at the public teachings I was giving in Montreal, and we would talk about her evolution. I highly recommended she take the necessary medication to help her, to not judge what was necessary for her, and mainly, to avoid any relapse, if possible.

Mounina agreed to take her medication to feel better and continue her evolution—her inner healing. Over time, as she was training with me and other members of my team, I could observe how much Mounina was evolving in accepting the physical imprisonment this disease can create, but mostly in recognizing the emotional and mental symptoms imprisoning her life force. I witnessed her transformation, her choices, her courage, her love, and her inner healing.

Mounina was taking more and more the individuation path, recognizing herself to the point of writing a very poetic book describing her learnings and her evolution with MS.

I hope this book will be a source of inspiration for all, as is its author Mounina. May you be inspired by its poetry and its depth, and do not hesitate to share it with others.

Congratulations, Mounina.

With love,
Marie Lise Labonté

Questions

Can I open myself to the possibility of an Infinite Loving Intelligence guiding and orchestrating this whole universe?

Can I listen to the wisdom of my divine body?

Can I allow the wisdom of my emotions?

Can I receive the wisdom of my conscious and unconscious mind?

Can I trust in the divine wisdom of my soul?

Blessing

May all beings be healthy, happy, holy.
May all beings be peaceful.
May all beings feel the simple joy of being alive.
May all beings be free from suffering.

The Guest House

This being human is a guest house.
Every morning a new arrival.
A joy, a depression, a meanness,
some momentary awareness comes
as an unexpected visitor.
Welcome and entertain them all!
Even if they're a crowd of sorrows,
who violently sweep your house
empty of its furniture,
still treat each guest honorably.
He may be clearing you out
for some new delight.
The dark thought, the shame, the malice,
meet them at the door laughing,
and invite them in.
Be grateful for whoever comes,
because each has been sent
as a guide from beyond.
—Rumi

Introduction

This true story tells my very personal journey from being very sick to being healthy, healed, and whole. This book is my journey of transformation from separation to union after a diagnosis of multiple sclerosis. This is my very personal and unique way to health. We are all different. The *challenge* is to honor our own unique paths.

Looking back now, I can only see Infinite Intelligence guiding my every step. I did not plan any of this. I simply could not have, even though my ego would certainly like to take the credit. I can never give myself a diagnosis of multiple sclerosis, and I can't heal myself from multiple sclerosis. I can only allow myself to heal. Infinite Intelligence can do it all! I feel humble.

Something much greater than me, much more powerful than me, and much more loving than I could ever be is at play. I like to call it life, lovingly, my queen. I am only learning, more and more every day, to surrender to her. It was all perfectly and divinely orchestrated.

Everyone is different and unique. We all are spiritual beings, having a brief and precious human experience. May we honor our unique paths. May we love and respect ourselves, each other, and this precious life.

Everything in this book is about what I learned in the past and what I continue to learn today. This book is a love story. This book is about how I fell in love with myself, how I fell in love with my body, and how I fell in love with life! This book is to invite you to fall in love with yourself, fall in love with your body, and fall in love with life! This book is divided in three main sections. I believe healing requires three essential steps.

The first step in healing is *acceptance* of whatever life brings to our doorsteps. This is easy to say, but in truth, it is a learning journey. It requires patience and compassion toward ourselves. It certainly did not happen all at once for me. It is an ongoing process. Acceptance is an essential step to move forward. It is so important. It is not easy, but it is crucial! I believe acceptance is the first step to move through any situation.

The second step in healing is *change*. We literally become someone else. The disease was in one version of the person. We become a new person—we become our authentic selves. We change as a whole—we change our bodies, our emotions, and our minds, thus changing our energy and raising our vibration.

This second step is unique to each person. I believe we all need to change. What and how we change is unique to each person. The symptoms of multiple sclerosis are unique to each person. We don't find two same manifestations of the disease. I believe each person has something unique to heal and to change. Each person gets a specific message relating to her or his own individual life. There are some commonalities, as well as some specificities.

The third step in healing is *forgiveness*. We release the past. In this last step, we move forward free from the past. We create a new future as a new person.

These three steps become a way of being. We accept and allow life now and forever after. We flow with life because life is change. We forgive. This is my new way of being. Again, and again I accept, I allow, and I love life. I go with the flow of life, and I forgive.

SECTION 1

Acceptance

CHAPTER 1

The Worst Thing That Happened to Me

How Could This Happen to Me?

My Outer Life Before and My Inner Life Before

From an outside point of view, I have lived a normal life. I was working full time for an actuarial firm. I had completed a bachelor's degree in mathematics. I was always very rational. I was halfway through the long and difficult process of becoming an actuary. I was working during the day. I was also studying in the evening and on weekends for actuarial exams.

I was what you could call healthy, being rarely sick. I ate pretty much anything. I had recently started practicing yoga. I had a lovely family, a loving boyfriend, and some friends with whom I would spend quality time. I would also enjoy my time alone. I grew up with a passion for books. I was always very curious.

But on the inside, I felt like a zombie. I was like a robot. There was no life in me, it seemed. I felt empty. I had felt so unhappy for as long as I could remember. I felt disconnected from my body. I felt disconnected from everybody. I felt disconnected from life.

My body was only a machine whose sole purpose was to get me from point A to point B—silently, please. I did not think my body had any intelligence. I had no emotions whatsoever. I am a strong woman. I considered emotions weak. So of course, I did not allow myself to have any. I was not aware of my thoughts—not one bit. I was completely unconscious.

I was numbing myself with marijuana and not allowing myself to feel anything. I did not want to feel anything. I was totally locked in and trapped in my rational mind. I was trying to find comfort in the logical view of life. I was viewing life through a very rigid black-or-white paradigm.

Failed Attempt at Meditation

I was so unhappy that I decided to escape to Asia. I felt called to go to Thailand to learn meditation in a monastery. I knew nothing about meditation. The monks in the monasteries seemed so at peace. I longed for those peaceful feelings. I had a feeling my mind was the source of all my suffering.

I left everything in my Western life to go meet the sages of the East. I emptied my apartment. I quit my job. I left my boyfriend, my friends, and my family. In 2003 I went to southeast Asia with my dear friend Leïla. On the internet, I'd found Wat Ram Poeng, a monastery in northern Thailand. It offered ten-day silent Vipassana meditation retreats.

I had the shock of my life regarding how hard it could be to sit and do nothing. I could not do it, so I left the monastery after one day. What a disappointment that was for me. I had come all the way from Canada only to find out that I really could not be with myself. I was scared to be alone with myself while doing nothing. I felt so defeated. I felt really sad that I was such a stranger to myself.

Discovery of Yoga

Fortunately, I also discovered yoga during that trip. Yoga showed me how bliss was right here, accessible in every moment, as close as my breath! I had known nothing about yoga. I did not realize back then that stepping out of my mind and coming into my body was what created this blissful experience.

I took a few yoga classes. My first experience with yoga was with a beautiful woman. She had been practicing yoga all her life. Her mother was a yoga teacher. Her first classes must have been in her mother's womb. She really changed my life. It was in a beautiful resort on the island of Ko Pha Ngan in southern Thailand called the Sanctuary. It was very tiny and simple at that time. It has grown quite a bit since.

I fell in love with this yoga practice that had the power to take me out of my mentally created suffering into the paradise of this present moment. When I came back from southeast Asia, I was eager to learn as much as I could about this newfound practice that could bring me so much peace. When I get a strong feeling about something, I become really passionate and want to learn all about it.

What Is Yoga?

Yoga means "union" in Sanskrit. Yoga is the union of the body, the heart, the mind, and the soul. The physical postures work on the body. The breathing exercises work on the emotions or the heart. Meditation works on the mind.

Yoga also means the union of our individual consciousness with the universal consciousness. In truth, there is no separation! There is only the illusion of separation, created by our minds. The practice of yoga helps dispel this very persistent illusion.

Yoga is an amazing tool, and I love it. I will always deepen my practice of yoga. I will always practice some form of yoga, as this union is endless.

Sivananda Ashram Yoga Retreat, Bahamas

In 2004 I went for a monthlong yoga retreat at the Sivananda Ashram Yoga Retreat in the Bahamas. I practiced karma yoga. It is the yoga of selfless action. That was quite a precious and powerful initiation to yoga. I practiced daily yoga postures, breathing exercises, chanting, and meditation. I also attended nightly talks on the philosophy of yoga.

With this program of karma yoga, I spent a month at a reduced cost to learn about yoga. In exchange, I worked for five hours every day on mundane tasks like cooking, cleaning, gardening, and painting. However, I mostly worked in the kitchen. Something magical was happening in that kitchen. I normally don't like to cook that much. But in that kitchen, I could cook for all the guests who came to this exotic yoga vacation. And believe it or not, the guests were telling me my food was good!

One day I was cooking with one of the resident senior yogis. He was cooking and at the same time repeating a mantra out loud. "Om Namah Shivaya." I learned later this is the mantra of transformation.

This was very disturbing to me at the time. I never imagined entertaining something other than my mental chatter. Instead of my usual negative self-talk, I saw someone controlling his mental activity. He was replacing it with something so much more beautiful, beneficial, and powerful. I was shocked and full of judgment. I did

6

not understand his wisdom at all. That senior yogi certainly knew better. Instead of letting his mind wander, he would master it using a mantra.

Kundalini Yoga Teacher Training Course

Back in Montreal, I began exploring different styles of yoga. I always felt wonderful after a yoga class. Sometimes I would practice a backbend, like the posture called the camel, and I would cry. Backbends are meant to open the heart. Or I would do a meditation to open the heart and would be moved to tears. I did not know why this was happening, but I felt relieved after the class. I did not give it much thought.

I was passionate and enthusiastic about this yoga practice, so I decided to enroll in a yoga teacher training course. I really wanted to deepen my understanding and practice of yoga. There are a lot of yoga teacher training programs offered in Montreal. In 2006 I enrolled in the first one I found: Kundalini Yoga Teacher Training Course, as taught by Yogi Bhajan. He is the famous yogi who brought kundalini yoga to the West. Kundalini yoga is the yoga of awareness.

Kundalini yoga is quite a complete form of yoga. It includes the physical postures called *asanas* in Sanskrit. They are quite challenging. They pushed me beyond my comfort zone, to say the least. I was in pretty good shape physically. I found the physical practices difficult, but I also found them beneficial.

Kundalini yoga includes breathing exercises called *pranayama*. I enjoyed having found something that focused my mind. I felt amazing counting my breaths and directing my breathing in a specific way.

Kundalini yoga includes meditation. Kundalini meditations are very powerful. They can include a hand posture called a *mudra*. A mudra helps guide the energy for a specific intention. The meditation can also include the mental or verbal repetition or singing of a mantra. A mantra is a word or sentence with a high vibration that has the power to transform the mind. In Sanskrit, *man* means "mind," and *tra* means "instrument." A mantra is an instrument for the mind.

I thought I had discipline. First, I studied to get a bachelor's degree in mathematics. After that, I studied for actuarial exams while working full time. But when the time came for the practices related to my yoga teacher training course, I had quite a lot of resistance. I could barely get myself to do the minimum required assignments. That was quite surprising for a person who had such a love for yoga and shocking for a person with presumed discipline. I hardly managed to get to the end of the training. I completed this two hundred–hour yoga teacher training course in June 2007 and became a certified kundalini yoga teacher.

First Crisis: Twenty-Ninth Birthday

On the very last day, I remember crying. I was feeling deeply sad that the training was ending. I felt I had found a precious gem. However, I had such resistance to the actual practice. I did not feel I had taken as much advantage as I could have.

So, I asked life to show me a way to this paradise of joy and peace. I was not living this paradise. I only knew it existed. I clearly remember asking the universe not to leave me to my ordinary existence and to show me a deeper meaning to life. I knew life could be much more than the three-dimensional material world I knew.

A few weeks after I became a certified kundalini yoga teacher, suddenly, within a few hours, the whole left side of my body became paralyzed. It was perfect—only my left side but my entire left side—my left leg, my left foot, and all my five left toes; my left arm, my left hand, and all my five left fingers. The left side of my face, including the left side of my lips and my left eyelid. I could not blink with my left eye. All the skin on the left side of my body felt different. I was too flabbergasted to have any reaction. I just watched in total awe while my body slowly shut down over a few hours. I was overwhelmed by this drastic symptom in my body.

I happened to be with my family at the time, and they immediately took me to the emergency room. After an MRI (magnetic resonance imaging) and a lumbar puncture, the doctors diagnosed me with multiple sclerosis, also called MS.

At first, I was shocked to realize that I even had a body. My body! What body? In reality, I was not so surprised by this pretty rapid diagnosis. I thought it was only normal because for so long in my life I had felt so unhappy. I had felt so empty inside for years. No one around me seemed to correlate what was going on inside me with what was happening in my body. I ignored it too.

I stayed in the hospital less than a week—enough time to be injected with massive doses of cortisol to diminish the inflammation in my brain. It worked miracles. In a few days, my paralyzed side slowly started to come back to life as the inflammation in my brain subsided.

The neurologist at the hospital came to see me very regularly. He was monitoring my every change. Each time he would ask me, as part of the neurological exam, to touch my nose with my left hand. Obviously, I could not. Not since the last days and not for the following weeks. I was so struck by the absurdity of the situation that each time he came around and asked me for the impossible, I would laugh hysterically at the irony of the situation.

With my whole left side unresponsive, I wondered how it used to be before when I could use it so unconsciously. I realized that I used to have no awareness at all of my body. Now I was wondering what to do with my left arm. What did I used to do with it? Where was it? How did I place it in space? How could I have lived all those years without realizing I have a body? I began to realize how locked in my mind I had been.

My body had always been a tool for me instead of a living, divinely intelligent miracle. It was an instrument I would do anything to quiet down. I had no idea it had an intelligent language. I had never imagined it could speak to me.

I really had to make an unbelievable effort to try to lift my left arm when I started physiotherapy a few days later. Lying in my hospital bed, I felt powerless with nothing to do. I remembered the tools I had learned in my yoga retreat a few years earlier. I began visualizing myself on the beach walking and scraping the wet sand with my moving left hand. I was feeling the sand under both my feet as I was walking on the beach in my mind. I would put myself to sleep by singing this song I learned during that retreat: "Day by day, in every way, I'm getting better and better."

I was in a wheelchair, but I was aware I was alive. I began to be grateful to be alive! Now that everything around me stopped, I had time to experience this beautiful feeling of simply being alive.

My dear friend Leïla would come to see me in the hospital. She told me that this dramatic event would split my life in two: my life before this horror happened and my life after. I certainly did not want to hear that. I wanted to believe that my life would go on just the same. This was so wise of her, but I was not ready to see it that way.

I remember seeing the shock and the sadness this diagnosis caused my friends, my family, and my boyfriend. They were seeing the result of years of suffering. All the messages I received were only regarding the negative side of this situation. Then everyone moved on with their lives.

Only one of my friends did not seem to be impressed by my current situation. Somehow Amelie Berthiaume seemed to know more than what I or anyone else knew. When I called her out of desperation from the hospital, she told me everything would be all right. I really wondered what she was talking about!

After a few days in the hospital, I was transferred to a rehabilitation center where I spent six long weeks. Coincidentally, this is where I spent my twenty-ninth birthday. At the time, of course, I did not see it as a coincidence. I was outraged by how unfair life was.

I worked very hard to go back to my life before this horror happened. I relearned every day-to-day habit that I used to do automatically and unconsciously. I learned to eat, to wash myself, to get dressed, to walk, and to talk. I even learned to tie my shoes again. I concluded the universe had made a horrible mistake. This was not supposed to happen to me. No problem—everybody makes mistakes!

I was determined to go back to my old life exactly as it was and to my old self exactly as I was. I even started smoking marijuana again without my neurologist's approval. I was in complete denial! I was not at all open to any message or meaning this dramatic event was offering me.

How could this happen to me? Why was this happening to me? I felt like a total victim of life and of myself. I really felt like I had nothing to do with this diagnosis. I felt like this was all happening to me. I really felt powerless.

My neurologist put me on a medication that was supposed to diminish the frequency and intensity of the relapses. I did not see any option other than taking a drug at that time. I began injecting myself every two days with a substance meant to lower my immune system.

Six months later, I went back to work part time. One day a colleague at work told me about her minister at her church and shared with me how this man had healed himself of multiple sclerosis. She even sent me an audio recording of him personally sharing his experience. *But I am not religious. I am rational*, I thought to myself. *And I don't believe I am sick*. I was in denial. I believed I was the victim of a horrible mistake from the universe, and as a result, I didn't hear the message my colleague was so kindly trying to pass on to me.

Sometime later, I participated in a support group for people newly diagnosed with MS. We all shared our own stories, and I received an insight. I told the group that maybe this was happening for a reason. Maybe this was to help us discover the jewel that was inside. I was shocked by my totally irrational sharing, and they all looked at me as if I were an alien. I even thought I was an alien myself! I soon disregarded that insight. I believed deeply that I didn't have the right to exist and acted exactly according to that belief, not listening to myself.

Listen to My Intuition

The worst thing that happened to me was clearly not listening to my intuition. Not listening to my body speaking to me through such a tragic symptom, not listening to the voice inside suggesting this diagnosis could help me discover the jewel inside, and not listening to the help that came my way through my colleague at work.

Intuition is a mental and spiritual faculty we all possess. It is our inner guidance system. It is our connection with the soul. Our soul connects us with Infinite Intelligence.

I had no idea whatsoever I had such a faculty. I was in the prison of my rational mind. Nothing outside this prison existed for me. As I was coming out of my prison, I learned about this gift of intuition. Very gradually, I learned my body is intelligent. I remembered I am a soul. I came to realize that there is an Infinite Intelligence guiding and orchestrating this universe and that I am connected to it. This is my healing journey of recognizing all the different parts of myself.

First, it was essential that I acknowledge this precious gift of intuition that I have. Now I listen to the messages I receive. This inner guidance is always loving. It is for my greater good and for the greater good of all.

Our inner guidance can come in many different forms:
- It often comes as a little voice inside—the voice of our hearts coming from the right side of the brain.
- It can come as an image.
- It can come as a physical sensation in our bodies.
- It can come in a night dream.
- It can come as a synchronicity.

There are practices and tools to help us connect with our inner guidance:
- We can practice heart-brain coherence to contact it.
- We can use oracles, like the tarot or the I Ching, to access it.
- We can also use signs in nature or the world around us to tap into it.

In her book, *Mind Over Medicine: Scientific Proof That You Can Heal Yourself*, Dr. Lissa Rankin calls our intuition our inner pilot light.

In her book, *Uncharted: The Journey Through Uncertainty to Infinite Possibility*, Colette Baron-Reid calls our intuition our first sense.

Follow My Intuition

It is essential we listen to our intuition. But to listen is not enough— we need to follow our intuition. However, following our intuition is not always easy. It certainly was not for me. It takes tremendous courage to follow one's intuition. I had to educate myself to learn the value of following my intuition. It certainly speaks to me. I am learning to listen, trust, and follow my intuition.

Our intuition can be the opposite of what our own rational mind would think. Our intuition can also be the opposite of other people's opinions. It can be really frightening to step into the unknown. It can generate a lot of fear to step out of conformity. It can lead to the road less traveled.

There is nothing more rewarding than to listen to our intuition. Our intuition is life speaking to us. The more we trust and follow our intuition, the stronger this connection becomes. The more we are open to receiving its messages, the more we will receive them. The more interested and aware we are, the more it will be available for us.

This wisdom is irrational. It does not come from our intellect. Our intellect cannot understand Infinite Intelligence. "Intuition is beyond logic," Osho says. We must not analyze it or fight it or argue with it. We just need to follow our inner knowing.

Getting to know our minds is important to develop this connection. Cultivating a quiet mind through meditation and practicing relaxation strengthens this connection. Regardless of whether we are in a relaxed state of body and mind, this information will find its way to our consciousness. It just makes the information come in a gentler way if we are relaxed and practice meditation.

The first time I heard my intuition was with my first physical symptom of MS. I was not in a relaxed state of body and mind. Because I never knew anything about listening to my intuition and had never listened, it came in a violent way that was hard to miss. Still, I ignored it at first. At that time, I did not know life could talk to me.

In life in general and particularly when it comes to healing, we need our intuition from the right side of our brains and our reason from the left side of our brains. We need all our faculties.

CHAPTER 2

Befriending Uncertainty

We Must Find Comfort in the Uncertainty of Reality.
—Chögyam Trungpa Rinpoche

My Own Illusion of Certainty and Control

Very quickly, the corporate environment obviously became too much for me. I could not concentrate surrounded by all the noise in the office. I was offered the choice to work from home. I felt devastated that I could not handle the work space. I felt excluded from society.

On my way home, I stopped at the bookshop. I bought a few of Pema Chödrön's books: *Comfortable with Uncertainty*, *When Things Fall Apart*, and *The Places That Scare You*. Those titles expressed exactly how I was feeling and what I needed to learn. I felt uncertainty had suddenly become a part of my life. I felt my world as I knew it had fallen apart. I felt living with this diagnosis was the scariest thing ever.

The first thing I began studying after I was diagnosed with MS was uncertainty. When we receive such a diagnosis, uncertainty becomes very frightening! What is going to happen? I learned that life is not more uncertain after a diagnosis of MS. But I became more aware that life is uncertain.

My life always seemed so certain. But from birth onward, there is really nothing certain about it. I never knew. I had never been aware of this fact. I had been living on automatic pilot. When I was young, I had decided my life was going to be very predictable. I was going to be in control. I was going to control every aspect of it. I wanted to control everything outside of me. I had no idea what was going on inside me.

Befriending Uncertainty

Uncertainty is an ordinary fact of life. Uncertainty is always present. Uncertainty never ends. Only death is certain. Timing is uncertain. I began realizing the illusion I had been living in: the illusion of certainty and control.

I resisted this basic fact. I denied it with every fiber of my being. I distracted myself so as not to face this basic truth. I spent a lot of energy trying to avoid uncertainty. I worked too much. I ate and drank too much. I became addicted to drugs and to the people around me. I did anything not to relate to life directly. I did all these things just to make sure I didn't get in touch with my inner life.

I was so blessed when I came across this amazing book, *Comfortable with Uncertainty*, by Pema Chödrön. It was love at first sight! She is a Buddhist monk. This book is about meditation and Buddhist wisdom presented in a very gentle way. Pema Chödrön is a gift to the world. I have found her books so precious.

I began getting comfortable with uncertainty by becoming curious about myself and about life and by realizing life is uncertain for everyone. With this book, I began learning the true meaning of uncertainty. Uncertainty is life. Life is like nature. We all know the weather is uncertain.

I began to relax with things as they were. It is very soothing for the nervous system to relax surrounded by uncertainty. All I could do was learn to get comfortable with uncertainty. I am indeed learning to find comfort in the uncertainty of reality.

Uncertainty versus Control

There is an important difference between uncertainty and control. Uncertainty is life. In her book, *You Can Heal Your Life*, Louise Hay writes: "The Only Thing You Ever Have Any Control of Is Your Current Thought."[1]

The only thing I can control is my inner state of being. My inner state of being is my thoughts and feelings. I can control my thoughts, which dictate my feelings, which in turn dictate my actions. The only thing I can control is myself. I can create paradise in my mind. I can also create hell. I choose. "We create our own inner weather," Mary Morrissey says so beautifully. Our inner weather is our thoughts and feelings.

During the summer of 2012, I was in my backyard in Montreal sunbathing. That day I felt my life was really paradise. The very next day, I felt my life was really hell. But nothing changed outside of me. Only my thoughts about my situation changed! This drastic realization made me wonder about the power of my thoughts. I started realizing that the only thing I can control is my mind.

I also have control of my reaction to "whatever life brings to my doorstep," as Gregg Braden says so poetically. I don't control the weather, and I don't control life. Nothing is under control. However, I certainly can control my reaction to the weather and to life.

This is very hard to accept, especially when I hate what I unconsciously created! I don't want to hear that I have anything to do with my disease and my life. My first reaction when I heard this was to feel guilty. I felt guilty for many years out of ignorance, but I learned. "Knowledge is power. A lack of knowledge is a lack of power," Dr. Bruce Lipton says.

I am not guilty or a victim. I am a responsible cocreator. When I was able to move past this guilt, I got to a place where I realized I am responsible. With responsibility, comes great power! This is huge. This changes everything.

I have the power to change from the inside out. Whatever I created—for instance, MS—I can transform. This does not mean I consciously created MS—not at all. This is so important. I did not consciously create my disease, but I can take responsibility. I can create health!

This is when I remember to be kind and loving with myself. I can be gentle with myself on my journey to change from the inside out. I remember those wise words from Lao Tzu: "The journey of a thousand miles begins with a single step."

Change Is Life

Life is change. In fact, change is our nature. We can look at nature for a model. Nature changes every moment. We and nature are the same. Not only is change possible; change is inevitable. Change is constant. Change has been my greatest interest for as long as I can remember. I have always been so curious about my potential for transformation. Why? Obviously because I wanted to change so badly!

In my early teens, I suffered from an obsessive-compulsive behavior with a fancy name: trichotillomania. Simply put, I had the compulsion of pulling out my eyelashes and eyebrows. It made me feel so unhappy, and I really thought I was possessed. I began wondering if change was possible for me. I also smoked tobacco and marijuana passionately in my teens. Some years later, I wanted to quit. I found that change was so difficult that it seemed impossible.

Years later, after a diagnosis of MS, I kept pursuing my passion: yoga. I found that if I could breathe, I could practice yoga. So happily, I did both: I breathed consciously and practiced yoga. Vigorous yang yoga was physically impossible for me at that time. Yang is about becoming. I was fortunate to discover the gentle practice of yin yoga. Yin is about being.

There are three steps to practice yin yoga:
1. Find your comfortable edge in the posture. This appropriate edge is where you stretch just beyond your comfort zone. It changes all the time; it is always new.
2. Stay still and surrender.
3. Stay there for a while: three to five minutes. This is the time to get to know your mind, to develop your focus, and to awaken the observer in you.

I learned yin yoga during a weeklong workshop with Sarah Powers in 2008. That same year, I also did another yoga teacher training course: Mind and Meditation, Level 2 Kundalini Yoga. These two trainings gave me evidence that I could, in fact, change. They pointed me to the fact that change belongs to the realm of the mind. If I can change my mind, I can change my life.

I used to think meditation was impossible for me. However, I found that sitting still for short periods of time and watching my mind was, as a matter of fact, possible. What a revelation to discover I could, in truth, change. What a relief to discover that I am not fixed in a certain way. Eventually, I quit smoking, and I stopped my obsessive-compulsive behavior. But I have free will, and I can resist change. By thinking the same thoughts over and over again, I am sure not to change.

First, I became aware of the stories I tell myself repeatedly by awakening the observer in me. Then, I started changing my self-talk by choosing to tell myself what I wanted. When I choose my conscious thoughts, my subconscious mind will start believing what I tell it. My subconscious mind has no sense of humor. It must accept anything I tell it. It cannot differentiate between what is real and what is imagined.

CHAPTER 3

The Best Thing That Happened *for* Me

A Miracle is a Shift in Perception in Me That Removes
a Barrier in my Awareness to Love's Presence.
—A Course in Miracles

Kripalu Yoga Teacher Training Course

I started teaching kundalini meditation. I love sharing what I love! I was also working part time from home. I felt calm coming back into my life. At this point, I thought I was complete in my recovery. I had done everything possible to recover after this crisis.

I felt my passion calling me back. My love for yoga was still the same, maybe even stronger than before. I needed a gentle style of yoga to fit my presently fragile body. I felt kundalini yoga was too vigorous for me at that time. I began searching for a gentler yoga teacher training course. In 2009 I found a kripalu yoga teacher training course. Kripalu yoga is the yoga of compassion.

I felt good immersing myself in this training. It felt amazing to be doing what I loved, surrounded by like-minded people. It felt wonderful using my body while doing the yoga poses I was learning. I love learning about the yoga philosophy and find it all fascinating. I really resonate with this practice of yoga. In June 2010, I completed this second two hundred–hour yoga teacher training course and became a certified kripalu yoga teacher.

My Tensed Body

After my first crisis, I would regularly get body massages. I had found an excellent massage therapist named Danielle Tremblay. She told me my body was holding a lot of tension. She introduced me to Marie Lise Labonté. This woman had created a holistic body and mind approach after having healed herself of a so-called incurable disease.

I myself had been diagnosed with a so-called incurable disease. I still denied I was sick and believed this had just been a horrible mistake from the universe. My massage therapist still got my attention, despite my profound denial. I grabbed one of Marie Lise Labonté's books where she describes the method she had created. It was love at first sight!

In her book, *Au cœur de notre corps: Se libérer de nos cuirasses*, Marie Lise Labonté describes the eight types of tensions that we can store in our bodies. These tensions are unconscious and begin in your mother's womb (more about that in chapter 6).

It is very simple: I really felt I had them all. Not one or two but all of them! At that point, I realized perhaps I was sick. Perhaps I was very sick! I literally devoured her books in a few days. I really fell in love with what I was learning, and I really wanted to meet this woman in person.

Dominican Republic: Opening Beyond My Rational Mind!

In 2010 after my kripalu yoga teacher training course ended, I agreed to participate in a study on multiple sclerosis that my neurologist was conducting. After going through an MRI as part of his studies, my doctor informed me that the results were not good and that I should try another medication. My current medication did not seem to be helping. I told him I needed some time off medication before starting the new treatment.

As it happened, at that exact time, I had planned to fly to the Dominican Republic by myself because I wanted to meet Marie Lise Labonté who was presenting her seminar: The Silence Within. I did not know much about this woman. I only knew she had created a holistic body and mind approach after having healed herself. I had started to read her books on the body and the unconscious mind. It was all fascinating to me. It was within the realm of what I could accept. It was within the familiar ground of what I thought I knew.

I found the seminar captivating. I learned things I did not even know existed. I was introduced to the practice of listening! *Interesting idea*, I thought. One evening after a day of teaching, Marie Lise Labonté told us she is a medium and would be going into a trance. A medium channels information from another dimension. She channeled beautiful messages for us—messages filled with love, empowering messages. I did not expect channeling. That was not part of the reality I knew. My rational mind had never heard anything outside this three-dimensional reality most of us live in.

I found out that I had been living trapped in a limited reality. I was allowing only what I could perceive with my five senses. My belief was: if I can see it, I can believe it. Over the years, I have found this belief is more empowering reversed: I will see it when I believe it!

Second Crisis: Thirty-Second Birthday

The night after the channeling, I had a dream. A voice in my dream clearly said to me: "You are healed!" The very next morning, I woke up to what would be the beginning of my second MS crisis. So ironic! My unconscious mind, the part of me that creates my night dreams, has a deep sense of humor! Of course, I did not see any comedy at that moment. I did not know what was happening.

My equilibrium had been injured. I had lost all sense of equilibrium. I could not even stand up. My coordination had also been harmed. I was seeing double because the image each eye was producing was not coordinated. I lost my abilities to speak and to write. This time, my cerebellum, the center for equilibrium and coordination, was damaged.

Far from home, alone, and completely helpless, I surrendered to life. I had no other choice than to surrender to what was happening. I had to let go completely. This crisis was way too much for me to handle. Little me was overwhelmed by this situation. I handed the power over to life. "I cannot handle this on my own," I told life. "You handle this!"

I was blessed. I had support and inspiration surrendering to life. In my mind, I was not arguing with my reality. First, I had just met Marie Lise Labonté, who had faced and overcome an incurable illness. She inspired me to do the same. She opened me up to the fact that I had a choice in my response to what was happening. I could either choose to close myself up or choose to open myself to what was, in fact, already here. She now lives in a totally different reality than the one most of us live in. Meeting her had created the tiniest opening in my mind that perhaps there is more to this disease.

Also, this dream I had the night before telling me "You are healed!" was so vivid that it was hard for me to completely believe what my body was showing me. It made my tragic circumstances seem less real than they appeared. A little corner of my mind was open. Could this disease be healing?

In my mind, there was an infinitely small opening for me to believe in more than my current condition. Those two events helped me surrender and let go of the way I thought life was supposed to be.

In the city where I was in the Dominican Republic, there is no terminal from which to board the plane. We were supposed to climb the stairs from the ground to board the plane. Obviously, I could not, as I was not even able to stand up. I had to board the plane to Montreal lying down on a stretcher. It was a very disturbing experience. Once back in Montreal, I was able to get out of the plane using a wheelchair. I went straight to the emergency room. Again, I ended up in the hospital on my birthday. I thought it was an odd coincidence that this had happened twice. I wondered why I had ended up at the hospital for my birthday again (more about that in chapter 11). I did not linger long in that space of wonder. Pretty quickly, I returned to being upset and sad.

Surrender

This time I learned my greatest lesson of all: surrender. This is very humbling. I am not in charge of life. Life is in charge! This time, I chose to open myself to the meaning of this diagnosis. I chose to begin to allow my life to fall apart. I chose to begin to accept that this was, in fact, happening.

The best thing that happened for me was awakening to the higher power of life and surrendering to her! I began learning to surrender more and more every day to life. I will forever deepen my willingness to trust and surrender to life. I began realizing there had to be a higher power in charge.

Over time, I learned that everything happens with mathematical precision. There is no coincidence and no mistake. There is nothing random about life. Life is perfect! There is an Infinite Loving Intelligence in charge of this universe. There is an Infinite Intelligent Love guiding and orchestrating this universe. Every moment there is only Infinite Intelligence happening. Life is perfect in all its perceived imperfection.

I had studied surrender as part of the yogic philosophy. It is called *ishvara pranidhana*, and it is one of the five observances, along with purity, contentment, self-disciple, and self-study. I had learned surrender intellectually. While in the Dominican Republic, I experienced it firsthand. There was nothing I could do. I had to accept life with all its horror. That was the most humbling experience ever! I am not in charge of the universe. I don't make life happen. Life happens. There is no arguing with life. She is always right! I never wanted to surrender my ego. I thought: "I will make it happen. I will be in charge."

What an illusion—a very limiting one. I had to let go of my will to make things different. I surrendered. I accepted to let go of control and let life take over. I began my lifelong journey of learning to surrender to life, so I began to relax and trust life. I began learning that being a partner with life is much more powerful than my own limited will. Now, I first set an intention for what I want. Then, I work as well as I can with the expectation of obtaining my intention. Finally, I surrender the result. It will happen: probably not on my terms, but on life's terms.

Surrendering is welcoming life.
Surrendering is the willingness to listen to life.
Surrendering is relaxing in the present moment.

Surrendering is being available and receiving life.
Surrendering is not resisting or ignoring but allowing life.
Surrendering is very frightening to my ego or my personality.
Surrendering is opening to the unknown and to the mystery of life.
Surrendering is letting go of myself and the way I think life should be.

Listening

The first step in healing and for life in general is listening. I did not know anything about listening until I was introduced to this powerful practice by Marie Lise Labonté. Listening is a skill with a beginning but no end. I can always refine this skill. I can always go deeper. I did not know my body could speak. I did not know I had an intuition that could speak. I did not know life herself could speak. I did not know life was alive and so precisely intelligent and loving.

I began listening to what is obvious: my body. My body is divinely intelligent and never lies. Its symptoms are not random and deliver a precise message. Nothing is random in this universe. Before I can listen, I must allow life to happen. Allowing leads to listening. Only when I allow whatever is happening to happen, can I begin to listen.

To listen is to be humble. To listen is to give up my illusion of control. It is to recognize I don't control life. To listen is to love. To listen is to know and trust that whatever is happening is in truth happening for my highest good. I listen with total acceptance. I listen with complete nonjudgment. I listen with an open and receptive attitude.

I listen with the right hemisphere of my brain. The right side of my brain is the yin side of myself. The yin side of myself listens. The left side of my brain is the yang side of myself. The yang side of myself acts. Yin and yang form a complete whole. I need both aspects in healing and in life in general.

Perception

At first, when I was diagnosed with MS, I thought that was the worst thing that could ever happen to me. In truth, the worst thing that ever happened to me was clearly not listening to my intuition.

Years later, I learned a lot. I did a lot of work on myself to transform myself. Then I thought this diagnosis was the best thing that happened to me because it ultimately led to my healing. In truth, the best thing that happened for me is surrendering to life!

Now, I think MS is just something that happened. Not the worst, not the best—just a part of my life's journey. Reality just is. Everything is neutral. I assign meaning to situations, conditions, and circumstances.

Perception is a mental and spiritual faculty we all possess. It is our point of view. We can give meaning to any situation. We can choose our reaction to whatever comes our way.

Truth be told, our reaction to any event is not even our own. We might think it is. It is, in fact, based on our conditioning: our family, our culture, and society. It is based on the way we learned to view life. It is based on our unconscious programming. It is not really our point of view. It is the point of view shaped by the world around us.

I must admit that I do not know if something is good or bad from my limited human perspective. I am learning it is so much more empowering to withhold judgment. Not judging allows me to remain open so the good in any situation can reveal itself to me. Nothing is only good or only bad. We live in a world of duality. Everything comes with its opposite.

Pema Chödrön teaches us in this quote: "Letting there be room for not knowing is the most important thing of all. When there's a big disappointment, we don't know if that's the end of the story. It may just be the beginning of a great adventure. Life is like that. We don't know anything. We call something bad; we call it good. But really we just don't know."

It is human to quickly judge. It helps me move through a situation if I pause my internal judgment and become curious. From the point of view of my soul, everything is neutral. From spirit's point of view, nothing is good or bad.

CHAPTER 4

Human Being

If you Can Cease all Restless Activity, Your
Integral Nature Will Appear.
—Lao Tzu

Retirement

While I was in the Dominican Republic in 2010, I had my second relapse. I had to come face-to-face with the realization that my memory had been affected. Not only was my physical body severely damaged but my mind was as well.

This was quite a challenging fact for me to face. Even my neurologist did not really believe me. Physical damages are undeniable. They are out in the open and can be seen immediately. Brain damage that affects memory is much more insidious.

Brain damage that affects physical ability, like walking, can be addressed. We have a well-established system that can help us do that, from physiotherapy to ergotherapy. Depending on the kind of brain damage, we can at least try to walk again. So, I did learn to walk and talk for the third time in my life!

I also began a new treatment to try to lower the frequency and severity of the relapses. My neurologist had me choose between two different types of medications, and so I picked the one with the fewest side effects. This time, I thought maybe there was something I could do to help myself and didn't feel as powerless as the first time. I had a dream telling me "You are healed!" and I met a woman who showed me healing was possible. So, I agreed to take the new medication while I was exploring what else was possible.

Brain damage that affects cognitive abilities is much more difficult to address. To address memory problems is a whole other story. I chose to devote my time and energy to figuring out what was happening. What was the meaning of this chaos?

My neurologist sent me to a neuropsychiatrist. I told the neuropsychiatrist this diagnosis could be the beginning of a grand adventure. She saw that I was not depressed or crazy, although perhaps a little extravagant.

My neurologist also sent me to a neuropsychologist. After many tests, she concluded my memory had been affected. I was incapable of doing the actuarial work I used to do. All my actuarial knowledge had been erased from my memory.

Turns out, I was sane! But doing my usual work would be impossible with my kind of brain damage. I even did a testimonial for my neurologist and his colleagues and students to testify about my brain damage. That was an intense experience. I felt so ashamed! My sense of worth was completely tied into my ability to do my work. If I was not an actuary, who was I? My sense of identity was totally tied to what I was doing. I felt crushed!

I know it is common for human beings to define ourselves by what we do. I used to work in pension plans. I would calculate people's pensions when they retired. Often, I would see in my database that people die soon after retirement. This had always made me so sad. People work their whole lives, wishing and waiting for the best time of their lives to come. When the time finally arrives, they die.

Why is that? Because it is unbearable to feel useless. Because it is heartbreaking to feel like we don't matter. Because it is intolerable to not know who we are anymore. Because we stopped doing what we did, and that was all we knew about ourselves. So, I knew that could happen when a person stops working. And that was exactly what happened to me. I felt devastated. For many years, I struggled with this until, very gradually, I was able to shift my sense of identity.

Sense of Identity

Who am I? Am I my name? Am I the daughter of my mother and my father? Am I the friend of this person and that person? Am I the wife of this man? Am I a mother? Am I my body? Am I a woman? Am I a Canadian or a Mauritanian?

Am I my thoughts and beliefs? Am I the voice in my head? Am I the emotion I am feeling right now? Am I an emotion I memorized that is stored in my body? Am I the story of my life? Am I a disease or a diagnosis? And above all for me in this instance: Am I my job? Am I my title? Am I my role? Am I what I do? Am I what I have? Who am I beyond all these identities?

What we identify ourselves with consists of an endless list. For many years, I suffered from the loss of my identification with my job. For so long, I did not know who I was. Through meditation, education, and self-study, I connected with the simple but profound joy of being. I discovered that I did not need any identification to exist. I Am. Just being is enough. I exist. That in itself is the miracle. I started to feel grateful for the miracle of being alive.

I discovered a whole new way of living. I used to want to have, then do, and to finally maybe be. Now, first I am learning to be, then do, finally have, and even give. From being, anything else can be added.

What Is Meditation?

I came back home from the hospital and stayed there. I was not working anymore. The first thing I learned was meditation. It is harder to understand our true nature as an infinite spiritual being of the universe with our intellect. It is easier to understand when experienced. The best way to experience it is through meditation.

But what is meditation anyway? Meditation is mind training— simple, but not easy. It is a practice to get to know our own thinking minds and to know we are not our thoughts. We are the space between our thoughts. We are the observers of our thoughts. "I am loving awareness," Ram Das says.

The first thing I discovered is that my mind is ever moving, just like the ocean. It is always in the past or future. It is full of distractions. A common name for the mind is monkey mind because it is always moving, just like a monkey. We all have monkey minds. We need to train our minds so they become "our servant instead of our master," Osho says. "The mind exists as a servant of the soul," Yogi Bhajan says.

I will always remember my first failed attempt at meditation in Thailand. It can seem like the most difficult, most boring, and most impossible thing to do at first. It certainly felt that way for me the very first time I attempted such a practice.

Meditation is an ancient and now scientifically proven practice. There is a gentle and gradual way to learn to meditate—no need to go to the other side of the world to do so. We can learn meditation right here, right now. Before meditation, there is concentration. There are many ways to develop our concentration. I started learning this way:

- I start in a comfortable position, sitting on the floor or in a chair.
- I close my eyes.
- I keep my spine straight and my body relaxed.
- I mentally count my breath from one to ten.
- I inhale, mentally repeating one. I exhale, mentally repeating one.
- I inhale, mentally repeating two. I exhale, mentally repeating two.
- And so forth, all the way up to ten.
- Then I count back down from ten to one.
- I inhale, mentally repeating ten. I exhale, mentally repeating ten.
- I inhale, mentally repeating nine. I exhale, mentally repeating nine.
- And so forth, all the way down to one.
- If I get lost in my count, and I do, perfect! I am normal—no judgment.
- I start over from the beginning.
- This is a process for training my mind.
- I repeat this process. It becomes easier with daily practice. It also becomes fun and is very relaxing!

This Too Shall Pass

Vipassana meditation is one of the oldest meditation techniques in India. *Vipassana* literally means to see things as they are in reality. It is a process of self-purification by self-observation.

There I was, in April 2012, with uncertain health and the life I had known destroyed by MS. I decided this was the perfect time to attempt another silent ten-day meditation retreat. This time I went an hour away from Montreal to the Goenka Vipassana Meditation Center. It became my first meditation marathon.

We would wake up at four o'clock in the morning to begin our first meditation. We would meditate for more than ten hours every day. We were not allowed to talk or read or write. We were not allowed to do any physical exercise. We ate very little.

This time I was able to sit in meditation for hours every day. It was anything but easy. It was painful at times in my body. It was boring at other times. It made me sleepy sometimes. It was also fascinating to spend so much time just observing. Nothing external could distract me. I could observe all my internal distractions, and they were unending! This was the perfect place to practice just being.

I experienced the first of the three universal truths of life: impermanence. Experiencing this truth was one of the most valuable lessons of my life. I was sitting still, trying to watch my breath as the air went in and out of my nostrils. I could observe how everything in my field of awareness was constantly changing.

Sensations in my body changed from one moment to the next. Emotions flowed through me like the waves in the sea. Thoughts came and went at an amazing speed like the clouds in the sky. Everything was changing. Only my awareness remained, unchanging. I am the observer of all the phenomena that constantly arises and falls away.

I came back home with a new mantra to put on my wall: "This too shall pass." If something unpleasant arises, I rest assured this too shall pass. So, I relax. If something pleasant arises, it's just the same—I rest assured this too shall pass. So, I relax and enjoy.

This teaches me to go beyond duality. It helps me develop equanimity—the ability to be with something, whatever it is. It's the ability to go beyond the mental labels of good or bad. It helps me welcome whatever arises. This retreat was the beginning of meeting and getting to know myself.

Buddha teaches us in this quote: "Praise and blame, gain and loss, pleasure and sorrow come and go like the wind. To be happy, rest like a giant tree in the midst of them all."

Impermanence, Egolessness, Suffering

I learned, in Pema Chödrön's book *Comfortable with Uncertainty*, that Buddha teaches there are three universal truths of life. These three characteristics describe us and our lives. To learn about these qualities and see their truths is to learn to relax with things as they are. Learning to relax in life in general and in the face of a diagnosis like MS is crucial.

The first truth of existence is impermanence.

Impermanence is an ordinary fact of life. Uncertainty and impermanence go hand in hand. Our bodies are ever changing. The body you were born into, where is it today? Every second, twenty-five million cells die. Every second, twenty-five million cells are produced. Our emotions flow through us. As the name implies, emotions are energy in motion. If we allow them to circulate, they will last only ninety seconds, according to Dr. Jill Bolte Taylor. Our thoughts are ever changing just the same. We have sixty thousand to seventy thousand thoughts every day, according to Dr. Joe Dispenza! Ninety percent are the same day after day. Over time, if we entertain the same thoughts, we keep living the same life.

The second truth of existence is egolessness.

It does not mean we let go of our personalities. On the contrary, I learned that we need strong and flexible personalities to live healthy lives. Egolessness means we have flexible personalities. It means we are curious, open, playful, and humorous. We don't take ourselves so seriously. We take ourselves lightly. If we are rigid and fixed, our personalities can keep us separate from each other and the world around us.

The third truth of existence is suffering.

We suffer because we resist the first truth of existence: impermanence. We resist the fact that life is constantly changing. We expect what is impermanent to be permanent; thus, we suffer. We resist the fact that we change and will die someday.

We suffer because we resist the second truth of existence: egolessness. We think we are a solid separate fixed individual, when the truth of our being is openness.

We suffer because "we mistake suffering for happiness," Buddha says. We think we will find happiness where only suffering can be found. For example, we think drugs and alcohol will make us happy when in fact, they can only make us suffer if we use them to escape reality. "We look for happiness in all the wrong places," Pema Chödrön says. We suffer when we look outside for happiness, while happiness is an inside job.

CHAPTER 5

Unconditional Acceptance

Accept—then act. Whatever the present moment contains,
accept it as if you had chosen it. Always work with it, not
against it. This will miraculously transform your whole life.
—Eckhart Tolle

Mindfulness-Based Stress Reduction

I had such a profound experience of just being during my ten-day
meditation retreat that I wanted to go deeper into the experience.
I kept practicing meditation. I kept reading fascinating books
about this ancient practice. There are many ways to meditate and
many definitions of meditation. Every religious tradition and every
spiritual tradition has its own. Even science has its own now.

In the Tibetan language, to meditate means "to become familiar
with." It is the process of self-observation. In Sanskrit, to meditate
means "to cultivate self." We can think of the mind as a garden. We
spend time removing the weeds and planting seeds. Meditation is
getting to know ourselves. Meditation on space is the latest style
I discovered with Dr. Dispenza in 2016. I became a student of his
work. I find it absolutely fascinating, and I love practicing this style
of meditation.

I would often read about a method developed more than thirty years ago by Dr. Jon Kabat-Zinn: mindfulness-based stress reduction (MBSR). I was thrilled to discover this eight-week course for adults who live with chronic illness. It was offered at the Department of Medicine at McGill University as a whole-person care program. In October 2012, without any hesitation, I jumped into this next experience.

Dr. Kabat-Zinn says: "Mindfulness is about being fully awake in our lives. It is about perceiving the exquisite vividness of each moment. We feel more alive. We also get immediate access to our own powerful inner resources for insight, transformation, and healing." It is a method that helps us fall in love with the present moment.

There are twelve attitudes for the foundation for mindfulness meditation practice, according to Dr. Kabat-Zinn, as described in this book *Full Catastrophe Living: Using the Wisdom of Your Body and Mind to Face Stress, Pain, and Illness.*

1. Nonjudging: Mindfulness is cultivated by assuming a stance of impartial witness to our own experiences. This requires that we become aware of the constant stream of evaluative and judging thoughts that we have—then step back. With a nonjudging mind, things are seen as neither good nor bad—but simply present or absent.
2. Patience: Patience demonstrates that we understand and accept that things have their own time for unfolding. We tend to be impatient with ourselves, expecting we should be able to calm the mind, stop the thoughts, or get over whatever is upsetting us. These things take their own time; the mind has a mind of its own, and patience allows us to simply observe the unfolding of the mind and body over time.
3. Beginner's mind: In order to be able to see the richness of the present moment, it helps to cultivate a mind that is

willing to see everything as if for the first time. We tend to become jaded and think we have seen or done this or that. In contrast, with a beginner's mind, the joys of the world as it unfolds around us become new again, as if we are all children—freed from our old expectations based on past experiences.

4. Trust: You are your own best guide. It is far better to trust your own feelings and intuition than to get caught up in the authority of experts. If at any time something does not feel right to you, pay attention, examine your feelings, and trust your own inherent wisdom.

5. Nonstriving: Meditation is different from all other human activities—we do it not with a goal or destination in mind but rather with a mind toward simply being—not doing. There is no objective other than to be conscious of yourself as you are.

6. Acceptance: Acceptance involves seeing things as they actually are in the present. We may not like it, but if that is the way things are, so they are. Acceptance allows us to cease struggling to change things that are beyond our ability to control and is the first step in any genuine process of change. Acceptance frees the mind.

7. Letting go: Letting go, also known as nonattachment, is fundamental to mindfulness meditation practice. In our minds, there are often things we want to hold on to (pleasant thoughts, feelings) or push away (unpleasant experiences). With letting go, we put aside the tendency to elevate some parts of our experiences and reject others—simply letting our experience be what it is, accepting things as they are without judging, and realizing the constantly changing nature of all experience.

8. Gratitude: The quality of reverence, appreciation, and being thankful for the present moment.

9. Gentleness: Characterized by a soft, considerate, and tender quality. Soothing; however, not passive, undisciplined, or indulgent.
10. Generosity: Giving within a context of love and compassion, without attachment to gain or thought of return. (The context of giving does not have to be material.)
11. Empathy: The quality of feeling and understanding another person's situation—their perspectives, emotions, actions (reactions)—and communicating this to the person.
12. Loving-kindness: A quality embodying benevolence, compassion, and cherishing; a quality filled with forgiveness and unconditional love.

These twelve attitudes were all very new to me. Now, however, I know they are attitudes I can cultivate and deepen throughout the rest of my life. There is no end to how deep I can go with them.

I share them all with you to show you the whole new world of possibilities that opened up for me with this MBSR course. It was a lot to take in at that time. I barely scratched the surface during my course. One of these attitudes really got through to me, and it was a major revelation. One of them planted a seed in me that blossomed by the end of the course: acceptance. It was life-changing!

Acceptance

We learned a lot of different mindfulness practices throughout this course. Some were formal, meaning we would dedicate a special time out of our daily schedule for the practice, which included mindful gentle yoga, body scan, and sitting mindfulness meditation. Others were informal, meaning they were to be practiced during the day as part of our day-to-day activities, which included mindful eating, breath awareness, and mindful walking.

At the end of our course, we learned by practicing together mindful walking. It simply consisted of walking very mindfully and completely conscious. We were being aware as we brought one foot up, being aware as we moved it forward, and being aware as we brought it back down. Very simple, but not so easy. We were practicing in quite a small room, walking around in circles. I could walk almost normally, but I would become tired very quickly.

One time we were practicing, and I felt myself becoming very tired with this walking. Instead of my usual reaction of going beyond my limits and not respecting my body's signal that it was enough walking, I unexpectedly completely accepted myself in the moment! I decided to stop walking and sit down on a chair. I began to listen to my body. I stepped out of the group to honor my need to sit down. I accepted that I was the only one who needed to sit down after such a short walk. I accepted to be different from everyone in the room. I felt proud and relieved to simply accept myself.

For me, that was a huge revelation! I can choose to respond with acceptance instead of ignoring my body and pushing beyond my limits. I never knew anything other than resistance. It was such an act of love from me to me. I had never even dreamed of giving myself such acceptance. It completely changed my life! I discovered the attitude of acceptance toward myself in the moment.

I saw that acceptance is an act of love. When I accept myself, I love myself. After the course was over, I began learning about acceptance and about loving what is. Slowly, I began to let go of my resistance to this powerful life. I always fought hard against what was. I exhausted myself fighting against what was. I often felt defeated battling against reality. Now reality was catching up with me. Reality was showing me even more than before that something needed to be heard and liberated. Something needed to change.

The Art of Allowing

Allowing is such a powerful skill! It is an attitude cultivated on the inside. It can sound very passive. On the contrary, it is a very active way of interacting with all of life—both one's inner life and outer life. Allowing may sound simple, but it is not easy. Allowing leads to listening. Before this diagnosis of MS, I did not know anything about allowing. I was all about resistance. I am learning to allow.

Allowing is saying yes to life.
Allowing is welcoming what is.
Allowing is opening to what is.
Allowing is simply receiving life.
Allowing is accepting and loving what is.
Allowing is being nonjudgmental toward what is and realizing it is not good and it is not bad; it simply is.

Accepting simply means it is that way right now. In no way does it mean I want it to be that way forever or that it should be. Byron Katie, author of the beautiful book *Loving What Is*, says: "Life is simple. Everything happens for you, not to you. Everything happens at exactly the right moment, neither too soon nor too late. You don't have to like it … it's just easier if you do."

In a deeper sense, allowing is raising my consciousness. Allowing is taking my power back. It invites me to realize I am at the center of my own experience. I am not a victim of it or guilty of it. I am 100 percent responsible for it. Allowing is the opposite of resisting. "What you resist, persists," says Carl Gustav Jung.

Nature knows no resistance. Allowing is what requires the least effort. I love that! Allowing is the opposite of fighting with reality. No amount of arguing with what is will change what is. What is, simply is. Our conditioning (our family, our culture, and society) can keep us from allowing, accepting, and loving what is. Our conditioning is the unconscious part of us.

Today, I know that allowing is the magic key that opens the whole magic of this universe. Only when I allowed my whole world to fall apart did everything start to change. Allowing opened the doors to transformation and healing. First, I allow, and I accept. Then, I realize this is here to teach me something. This is here to show me something I was unconscious of up until now. As scary as this might sound, I trust that if it is happening, I have everything in me to deal with it. Only by accepting what is happening can I move forward and grow with what has happened. The only way out is through. I have infinite gratitude for Marie Lise Labonté who introduced me to this powerful way of being. From the simple act of allowing, miracles follow.

Perfection

We live in a perfect universe. We live in a conscious universe guided and orchestrated by an Infinite Loving Intelligence. Allowing life to happen led me to begin to realize that life is perfect. Knowing now that life is perfect helps me to allow it to unfold more gently. In his beautiful book *Siddhartha*, Hermann Hesse writes: "The world is not imperfect or slowly evolving along a path to perfection. No, it is perfect at every moment, every sin already carries grace in it."

Before I was diagnosed with MS, I had no idea I was sick. MS came to heal me! It came to make me aware of what was oblivious to me. MS was the perfect vehicle for my evolution. Life reflects back what is in our unconscious mind and, thus, impossible for us to see.

It is very helpful to know that life happens with divine perfection. There are no random events, no coincidences, and no mistakes.

All is in divine grace. It is important to realize that life happens *for* us. Life does not happen to us, and we are not powerless victims. We are 100 percent responsible for our experiences, and we are powerful cocreators with life.

Since the day we are born, we are cocreators with life, whether we know it or not and whether we want to or not. That's just the way this vibrational universe works. Obviously, we begin as unconscious cocreators. We can learn to become conscious of our creative natures. We create with our thoughts, feelings, and actions, but most of our thoughts are unconscious. Jung teaches it is our nature to make the unconscious conscious.

We do not have to go looking for what is in our unconscious minds. It is perfectly reflected in our bodies and in our realities. We can work at creating something else if what we created is not to our liking. That is not always easy to accept. However, I believe it makes acceptance easier by knowing life happens for our highest good and the highest good of all. It is also very empowering to know that we have a say in the creation of our lives.

Every moment, there is always more right than wrong. We are breathing! Every moment is sacred. Everything that happens is exactly what is supposed to happen. It is exactly what we need for the evolution of consciousness.

In his beautiful, life-changing book *A New Earth: Awakening to Your Life's Purpose*, Eckhart Tolle writes: "Life will give you whatever experience is most helpful for the evolution of your consciousness. How do you know this is the experience you need? Because this is the experience you are having at the moment."

Thomas A. Edison said: "I know this world is ruled by infinite intelligence. Everything that surrounds us—everything that exists—proves that there are infinite laws behind it. There can be no denying this fact. It is mathematical in its precision."

As a mathematician, I love this mathematical precision of life. I certainly did not know this before my diagnosis. Now I am waking up to this fact.

SECTION 2

Change

CHAPTER 6

Miraculous Body

The Body Never Lies.
—Marie Lise Labonté

My Body Called for My Attention

After my mindfulness-based stress reduction course, I really felt a call from my body to get to know it better. It was my body that screamed so loud in order to get my attention. And it sure did: my whole world fell apart! The body practices of gentle yoga, body scans, and mindful walking resonated with me the most. I felt like I was giving my body some love as I was giving it some attention.

It was obvious to me that I had to listen to it now. In the past, I did not hear its gentle whispers, but I sure heard its loud cry. I felt it was only natural that I begin by paying attention to my precious body. In 2010 I had learned about Marie Lise Labonté from my massage therapist. After my second relapse and my physical rehabilitation, I went back to what had gotten my attention.

Now was the time to look into this holistic bodywork approach more deeply. So, in 2013 without any hesitation and without even investigating this method, I enrolled in a two-year training program in Montreal. It is more a deconditioning or an unlearning rather than a training. At the end of the course, I became a certified holistic bodywork practitioner.

From Machine to Miracle!

While I was in the training, we first had to learn about the anatomy of the body. To my amazement, I discovered we have more than six hundred muscles. I knew we had a few, but not that many. I never imagined! Our muscles are organized in layers. Each region of the body can have one or many layers: from the surface of the body to deep in the body. The skull has only one layer, while the back has many, for example.

We have more than two hundred bones. We have eleven systems all working in harmony to maintain the homoeostasis of our body. Our skeletal, muscular, nervous, endocrine, cardiovascular, lymphatic (immune), respiratory, digestive, urinary, reproductive, and integumentary (skin) systems keep us in equilibrium as we live our lives.

I started to realize that my body is not a machine. My body is, in fact, a miracle. Most of us don't realize our bodies are miracles. All the amazing functions they perform without us even being aware. It is divinely orchestrated. It is intelligent beyond human comprehension.

We can think that what gives us our every breath and every heartbeat only comes from our biology and our autonomic nervous system. We can reason it only comes from the systems, organs, tissues, cells, molecules, atoms, and subatomic particles. But from a quantum perspective, it is all energy—the same energy that makes up the whole universe. Who animates that energy if not an Infinite Loving Intelligence, as Dr. Dispenza reasons? The training had not officially begun, and yet I was already in a state of amazement for my miraculous body.

What Is Marie Lise Labonté's Holistic Bodywork?

This bodywork is intended to liberate the tensions and suppressed emotions from our bodies. A tension is created in our bodies when our reptilian brains perceive a threat or danger. This particular part of the brain then sends a signal to our muscles to contract. It is an unconscious process.

I learned that the body is the unconscious mind and that the body never lies. It expresses whatever is held in mind and keeps a memory of everything from the past. It is a blessing that we have a body to let us know what is impossible for us to see.

This bodywork is like a psychoanalysis of the body. Practicing this work is a time to listen to and liberate the memories and beliefs stored in the body. I religiously practiced this work over many years. Over time, it really unleashed my awareness of all the intelligence of my body.

The goal of this method is not to get rid of all tensions but to soften them. We want to be able to use these tensions when we need them and release them when we don't. These tensions serve as protection. They are sacred. Sometimes, we need to protect ourselves, but we don't want to be imprisoned by our tensions. They protected life in us when we needed it the most when we were babies. A relaxed muscle is always in a state of tension to counteract the constant effect of gravity. Some tension is normal. Muscle tone maintains posture.

The physical movements are practiced mostly lying down on the floor, very gently and very slowly. There are three types of movements: opening, stretching, and harmonizing. All types are included in one session. A specific region of the body is always targeted during a class. The tools used consist mainly of a tennis ball, a foam ball, a stick covered with foam, and a small cushion. The movements are mostly circles with an arm or a leg, rotations of the head, pelvic tilts, leg extensions, explorations of the zero point with an arm or a leg (the point with no gravity), or side openings.

Opening movements always begin a holistic bodywork class. The movements and the tools used with the movements allow external energy to come into the body. They also allow the energy located deep in the center of the body to come up to the surface of the body and be liberated. They help lubricate the joints and disentangle the connective tissues. They create space inside and outside the body. They are yin in nature. They activate the parasympathetic nervous system, which activates the relaxation response. They lead to the experience of no time.

Stretching movements always follow opening movements. They give a direction to the energy just released. They allow this energy to be communicated to the different muscular layers of the body. They are yang in nature. They are natural antidepressants. They are at the heart of a class.

Harmonizing movements always close a holistic bodywork session. They are very soothing for the different muscles after they have been opened and stretched. They work at bringing harmony and equilibrium between the left and right sides of the body and between the top and the bottom parts of the body. They integrate the different hemispheres of the body with the center of the body.

Over the years, my whole body frame changed. Not only did the movements release the tensions from my muscular system but they also released tensions from my skeletal system. My bones, cartilages, ligaments, joints, and connective tissues could now move more freely to regain their natural alignment.

It felt wonderful to give my body some attention and some gentle, loving care. It felt really good to make me feel good. I felt all the love I was giving myself. I felt as if my body was responding by loving me back.

At first, when I practiced the movements, it was very painful. In the beginning, I could not even practice some of them, and I had to visualize instead. I could not believe the pain I felt when I gently massaged a muscle. The day after a practice, I would wake up with my whole body aching. All my muscles were in pain as if I had done a vigorous marathon. I was shocked! How could that be? I had practiced lying down, and I was barely moving my body. These movements are almost invisible to the untrained eye, but still my body hurt as if I had practiced some extreme sport. The movements had such a powerful effect on my body.

I began realizing that my muscles had been really contracted. My body was more like a concrete cylinder. My muscles were so contracted that no life was able to get in or out of me. I had been living trapped in the prison of my contracted muscles. By practicing these movements, my prison was very slowly and very gently beginning to crack open and tumble down. Over time, the pain gradually subsided. Eventually, I would practice the same movements and experience pure pleasure.

Slowly, I began to feel life coming back into my body. Life was also allowed to come out of my body. I had felt constricted before. Now I started to feel more expansive and more spacious in my body. It felt amazing!

I began to breathe more completely and more fully. All my muscles involved in the breathing process began to be liberated. I could inhale more deeply as all the muscles involved in a normal inhalation could contract to create more space in my rib cage. Mainly, my diaphragm could contract more freely down, and my external intercostal muscles could contract to bring my rib cage up. I could also exhale more completely as these muscles could relax to let the air out, and my internal intercostal muscles could contract to bring my rib cage back down.

I felt liberated to allow more breath in me. Being able to let so much life in me is absolutely the most delicious feeling ever. I felt I was coming back to life! I began to have more energy from consistently practicing these movements. My energy lasted longer and renewed itself faster. I found I was not so tired anymore.

I felt I had found my body, and it felt awesome. I really started to live in my body. I don't just know with my head that I have a body; I experience it every moment. It felt wonderful to fully embody it.

I learned the power of gentleness. That was a radical shift for me. I used to be so rough in general in life, not just with my body. I discovered gentleness can be more powerful than harshness. I discovered the power of being gentle with my body and in life in general.

I learned that my body is far more intelligent than my rational mind, to say the least. It has the power and intelligence of life herself as it is alive. I learned that I can trust and listen to this precious divine miracle.

On a weekend near the end of our training, we practiced classes to liberate all the diaphragms of the body: pelvic, thoracic, collar bone region, and cranial. At the close of one of those classes, we were all invited to share our experience as usual. I heard myself share: "I am a vibration." This was no ordinary share because I was surprised by what came out of my mouth. I experienced the fact that I am a vibration and the concept of no time. Years later, I learned that we are indeed a vibration living in a vibrational universe.

Physical Tensions

Physically, in the heart of the body is the spinal column, all intrinsic muscles, and the central nervous system. Psychically, in the heart of the body is where the real identity and essence reside. It is where creativity, joy, love, healing, and light all live. Energetically, it is where the life force runs.

Also, we all have one fundamental wound at the beginning of our lives. It is one of the following wounds: abandonment, rejection, nonrecognition, betrayal, abuse, humiliation, injustice, or the obligation to be happy. This wound is physical and unconscious. It is connected to the life force and creates in us the impulse to die.

In this holistic bodywork method, there are eight types of tensions. The first four tensions are the deepest, and they are fundamental. We all have them to one degree or another. The other four tensions are more superficial and relate to our search to identify with something external.

The tensions are created in the following order and in the following regions:

1. The fundamental tension is in the ocular region: the eyes and the skull, which includes the forehead, the nose, the cheeks, and the ears.
   This tension begins in our mother's womb up to two years old. This first fundamental tension comes around our fundamental wound. It comes to protect us from the pain we feel from this wound. All the other tensions will be installed around the first fundamental tension, one on top of the other, like the layers of an onion.

2. The tension of helplessness is in the oral and neck regions: the chin, the throat, the occiput, the lips, the jaws, the tongue, and the muscles in the deep region of the neck. It is installed from two to seven years old.

3. The tension of the poorly loved is in the thoracic region: the intercostal muscles, the pectorals, the deltoids, and the arms muscles. It also includes the heart and the lungs. It is created from four to ten years old.

4. The tension of protection is in the diaphragmatic region: the diaphragm. It also includes all the digestive organs: the liver, the gallbladder, the stomach, the pancreas, and the spleen. It is installed from five to twenty-one years old. This fourth tension is installed to seal the other first tensions. These four first tensions seal our inner world. They make us lose contact with our inner world—our identities. We start to identify with the outer world.

5-6. The parental tension and the tension of belonging are in the abdominal region: the abdominal, the lateral, and back muscles. It includes the intestines and the kidneys.

This parental tension is installed from five to eighteen years old. The parental tension makes us seek our identities from our parents by imitating them or rejecting them.

This tension of belonging is installed from thirteen to twenty-one years old. We start seeking our identities with a group.

7-8. The narcissistic and social tensions are in the pelvic area: most muscles of the pelvis, the hips, and the legs.

The narcissistic tension is created from thirteen years old. It is all about appearance: appealing or repelling.

The social tension comes last, from thirty years old. It is all about conformity.

All this information is based on the work of Marie Lise Labonté. She was influenced by the vision of Dr. Wilhelm Reich, psychiatrist and psychoanalyst, and Ida Rolf who created Rolfing. For more details, please refer to her book: *Au cœur de notre corps: Se libérer de nos cuirasses.*

My Immune System

Suddenly, one day in 2013 I had an insight: *What if my immune system did not try to kill me by destroying my myelin?* The myelin is the coating around the nerves that protect it. It allows for the information in the nervous impulse to be carried along the nerves in a speedy manner. This is the part of the nervous system that becomes damaged with multiple sclerosis. *What if, instead, my immune system tried to save me from myself?* I thought it was an interesting insight, to say the least.

A year or so later, I read a quote in one of Louise Hay, Ahlea Khadro, and Heather Dane's books: *Loving Yourself to Great Health: Thoughts & Food? The Ultimate Diet.* They say: "Metaphysically, we feel that inflammation and chronic disease are really about your body loving you enough to give you a wake-up call. It's an *invitation* to listen to your body and return to a state of self-love."[2] My insight, which was on my immune system saving me from myself, began to make more sense.

I grew up in Africa for the first ten years of my life. Sanitary concerns are not an obsession like they are in the Western world. They are a luxury very few can afford. All my life I had rarely been sick, having developed such a strong immune system from growing up in a third-world country.

I had come across the medical concept of the hygienic hypothesis, which states that lack of early childhood exposure to infectious agents, symbiotic microorganisms, and parasites suppresses the natural development of the immune system. Epidemiological data show us that developing countries have a lower rate of autoimmune disorders.

I knew that I did not have a weak immune system. Actually, it is quite the opposite. When I was diagnosed with MS, I could not believe that suddenly my immune system had turned on me by attacking my nervous system. I did not know what was happening. But I could never believe I had a weak immune system—not after growing up in Africa.

The idea that my immune system was, in fact, trying to save me from myself made sense to me. When the whole left side of my body became paralyzed with my first MS crisis, my body did indeed relax to let life flow in and out of me again. It was quite a drastic way to get me to relax, but the extent of my imprisonment was also quite extreme. My muscles had been so contracted that they were sucking the life out of me.

Today, I know that my immune system did save my life. I also know that my immune system was weak after enduring years of stress and limiting emotions.

The Relaxation Response

The autonomic nervous system is part of the nervous system. It is responsible for activating either the sympathetic nervous system or the parasympathetic nervous system. The stress response is activated by the sympathetic nervous system when a threat or a danger is perceived. It is a life-saving response when we are in situations of danger and need to either fight or flee.

In a healthy body, stress is reduced when the danger passes. The problem arises when we are continuously in a state of stress. Imbalance begins when we are constantly activating the sympathetic nervous system. We know today that most diseases are stress-related and that all symptoms are made worse when stress is present. We can activate the stress response by thought alone. We can use our imagination to terrorize ourselves as if a tiger were about to eat us. In reality, there is no such threat.

To create balance in a healthy body, we must activate the opposite mechanism: the relaxation response. The parasympathetic nervous system is called the rest, digest, repair, and growth mode. "In such a relaxed state, the body can get busy doing what it does best—making an effort to heal itself,"[3] Dr. Rankin explains in her book *Mind Over Medicine*.

The relaxation response was discovered by Dr. Herbert Benson and his colleagues in the laboratories of Harvard Medical School and its teaching hospitals. Dr. Benson writes in his book *The Relaxation Response*: "After twenty-some years of refining my understanding of our remarkable physiologic capability, we found that the two essential steps to eliciting the Relaxation Response are:

1. Repetition of a word, sound, phrase, prayer, or muscular activity.
2. Passively disregarding everyday thoughts that inevitably come to mind and returning to your repetition."[4]

All forms of meditation tend to activate the parasympathetic nervous system. The parasympathetic nervous system constricts the pupils; stimulates the production of saliva; slows the heart rate and the breath; stimulates the activities of the stomach, gallbladder, and intestines; contracts the bladder; and promotes the erection of the genitals.

Activation of the parasympathetic nervous system decreases the stress-related cortisol hormone and replaces it with happy hormones, which include dopamine, melatonin, and serotonin. It allows the immune system to function at peak efficiency instantly and reduces the metabolic rate. It increases blood flow in the brain as well as the activity in the left prefrontal cortex (which is observed in happier people).

In her book *Mind Over Medicine*, Dr. Rankin gives a list of other ways to relax. She writes: "It's not just meditation that shuts off the stress response and calms the body. As we've learned, creative expression, sexual release, being with people you love, spending time with your spiritual community, doing work that feeds your soul, and other relaxing activities such as laughter, playing with pets, journaling, prayer, napping, yoga, getting a massage, reading, singing, playing a musical instrument, gardening, cooking, tai chi, going for a walk, taking a hot bath, and enjoying nature may also activate your parasympathetic nervous system and allow the body to return to a state of rest so it can go about the business of self-repair."[5]

A breathing exercise with the exhalation longer than the inhalation, also switches us to the parasympathetic system. We can inhale for the count of three and exhale for the count of six. We do this at least three times.

There are so many ways to promote a state of relaxation. The importance of relaxation can never be underestimated. Health requires balance between stress and relaxation. If the body is compared to a car, the sympathetic nervous system would be the gas, and the parasympathetic would be the break.

Not all stress is bad. There is a positive stress, which is a natural response or instinct to an alarm signal so we can be alert to what is happening. It depends on how we react to a situation. Stress can become negative if we don't deal with the threat, endure a situation for a long time, and don't do anything about it. This leads to burnout.

The Parasympathetic and Sympathetic Nervous System

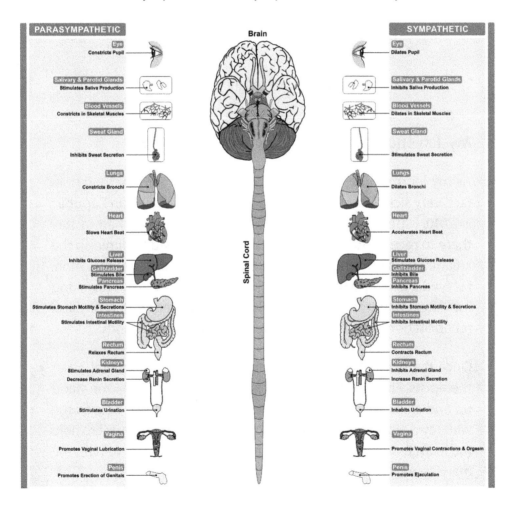

CHAPTER 7

Emotional Intelligence

Emotions Are Life in Me!

My Psychologist During My Rehabilitation

As my journey unfolded, I realized more and more that I was, in fact, very sick. After my second relapse in the Dominican Republic in 2010, I spent a month in the hospital in Montreal. I had to stay there to receive intravenous cortisol, which served to diminish the inflammation in my nervous system. I was also there for observation. I stayed there for what seemed like an eternity to be on a waiting list. After waiting four long weeks, I was transferred to a physical rehabilitation center where I stayed another whole month.

Once there, I had to see a psychologist along with several other therapists. First, I began seeing a physiotherapist to help me stand up and walk. Then, I had to see an ergotherapist who helped me with my day-to-day activities. I had to see a speech therapist to help me learn to talk again. I also had to see a social worker to help me manage my worldly affairs.

One day while I was talking with my psychologist, he asked me about my affects. I had no idea what he was talking about. He explained to me that these are my emotions. I still had no idea what he was taking about! Up until then, I had lived completely from my rational mind. I had a black-or-white paradigm for everything in me and in my life. I grew up valuing only my rational mind and considered emotions, like crying or laughing or getting mad, as weak.

Nothing could touch me. Nothing in me and nothing around me could get to me. I was very well protected under all my tensions. But I was not alive. I was like a zombie. I had no life in me, it seemed. I was a tough and very rational woman. I thought emotions were weak and irrational. So, of course, I did not want anything to do with weak, irrational emotions.

I did not allow myself to feel anything. I never cried. I spent years smoking marijuana, numbing myself. I thought it was safer to be in my head. I did not allow myself to laugh. I grew up with the belief that laughing was not allowed. To laugh I had to be either high or drunk. I thought there was nothing to laugh about in this life anyway. I believed there was no reason for joy in this life. I certainly did not allow myself to feel any anger. I grew up believing that anger was not a valuable emotion for a girl. I believed good girls don't get angry. I was a good girl, so I would never get angry. That day with the psychologist I had the shock of my life to learn there was a whole side of myself I had never allowed to exist. There was a whole dimension of myself I didn't even know existed.

The real beauty of this story is that in the symptoms I had following this second relapse, one of them was that I was overwhelmed with emotions. How ironic. I went from having none and not even knowing they existed to having too many. I would be oversensitive and cry like a baby about what was not that sad. I would laugh like a child at what was not so funny. Some days I would just be mad for no apparent reason. It felt like my emotions were really trying to reclaim their right to exist. Once I released the emotions stuck in my body, once I expressed them, once I allowed them to exist, they returned to normal—not repressed, not overwhelming, but a natural expression of life flowing through me.

Release Suppressed Emotions with Physical Movements

When I started liberating my body by practicing the movements of this holistic bodywork approach, a lot of emotions were liberated. Sometimes, I would massage my feet by rolling a tennis ball underneath them and find myself laughing uncontrollably. Nothing funny was actually happening, but it made me laugh.

Other times, I would massage my buttocks and hips and would experience a great deal of anger in the days that followed. Nothing in my current reality was actually upsetting me. I could not explain at that time all this frustration, but I was really mad.

At another moment, I would practice a movement to open up my chest, and tears would start running down my face. I would begin sobbing like a baby just from stretching my arms away from my body. Or I would lie on the floor on my back with a cushion under my heart and cry even though nothing was happening to justify this sadness.

I realized that all those years of not expressing my emotions resulted in them being stored in my muscles. They had been in my body all this time, waiting for me to recognize them, express them, and release them.

My body had been living in the past. When I had an unexpressed emotion, it became stored in my body. My body had been frozen in time. Liberating all those stuck emotions brought me back in the present moment. I had lost my body somewhere in the past and had found it again.

It must have been heavy to carry around all those emotions for so many years. I had never been aware of that burden. I just know that after releasing those emotions, I felt liberated and so much lighter. I felt like I had laid down heavy baggage I had been carrying around unconsciously.

Release Suppressed Emotions with Writing

When we are sad, for example, it is only a part of us that is feeling sad. We are so much vaster than an emotion. However, sometimes it can feel like every part of us is sad. Because the sadness can be so overwhelming, it can feel like we are only sadness.

During my holistic bodywork training, I also learned a technique to release an emotion when you are stuck and feel overwhelmed by this emotion. The emotion can feel like a prison, and nothing else seems to exist. It can become your identity.

When you feel an emotion is bigger than you, practice the following exercise to get out of the prison that the emotion represents. First, set a specific time to listen to the emotion every day. It's important to choose the same time every day because the unconscious mind likes habits. Pick a time when you won't be disturbed.

Second, you write whatever comes to mind without censoring yourself. Let the emotion completely free to express itself and listen to what the emotion has to say. If the emotion arises during the day outside the scheduled time, tell it to wait for the designated time and then honor the commitment by showing up for that appointment.

Do this listening and writing exercise for at least twenty minutes, up to forty minutes, every day. Don't read the writings; just burn or destroy the paper once you are done and thank your unconscious mind. You can do this exercise for two weeks or for as long you feel overwhelmed by that emotion. This is going to help express and release the imprisoning emotion.

Increase Positive Emotions

Emotions that are experienced can be divided into two categories, as classified by Dr. Dispenza in his book *You Are the Placebo: Making Your Mind Matter.*[6] We have the limited emotions associated with survival and stress. They are: "doubt, fear, anger, insecurity, worry, anxiety, judgment, competition, hostility, sadness, guilt, shame, depression, and lust". These emotions are more selfish. They belong to the first three energy centers.

We also have the elevated creative emotions that are more selfless. These are: "gratitude, love, joy, inspiration, peace, wholeness, trust, knowingness, presence, and empowerment." They belong to the fourth energy center. (Please refer to the chakra system image near the end of chapter 10.)

We want to be able to feel the whole rainbow of emotions, but we don't want a limited emotion to become an identity. First, we become aware of the emotions we are feeling on a regular basis. Then, we cultivate an elevated emotion by entertaining thoughts that create it. I work at ever deepening my capacity to observe and notice my mind and the emotions I am feeling in my body.

About Our Conditioning

We are conditioned beings. It is completely normal and natural. Our conditioning is the programs or paradigm in our unconscious minds. Of course, the first and most dominant conditioning we live by is the one from our parents or the person who raised us for the first years of our lives. We work at freeing ourselves from their influence. We don't want to be another version of them or their opposite. We simply want to be ourselves. This takes a lifetime because their influence is so strong and prevalent in our lives.

The unconscious mind becomes conditioned and programmed mostly in the first six years of life. From there, conditioning continues to grow. We can end up adults running programs that we would not choose and that don't serve us. This is where the problem begins. Transformation and healing lie in the unconscious mind—in the inner world.

This conditioning is information passed down from generation to generation. It begins in our genes and continues to develop in our environments. It comes from our families or our caretakers, from the cultures we were raised in, and the societies we grew up in. It comes from religion, education, politics, and the media. Conditioning is other people's habits.

We are conditioned from birth. When we are born, we are instinctive and wild creatures, and we need conditioning. This is perfect. It can be no other way. We live by the programs in our unconscious minds. In the first six years of life, we are like sponges. Our brain waves are in delta from zero to two years old and then theta from two to six years old. Those are the slowest brain waves. This means the unconscious mind absorbs everything with which we are presented. It must accept, believe, and surrender to everything without any analysis. There is very little conscious mind in an infant to analyze and reject any information. Only its inner world exists.

From six years old, brain waves speed up and go into alpha. The outer world becomes more real than the inner world. From twelve years old, brain waves become even faster and move into beta. We are then completely in the analytical mind. We are cut off from our unconscious inner world in beta brain waves.

Before six years old, the unconscious mind is wide open to the world around us. In delta and theta brain waves, we are super learners. We learn all the information we need to survive in this world. All this information becomes the beliefs by which we will live our lives. Most of our beliefs are formed in the first six years of life. All this information dictates what we will believe about anything and everything. It will govern all.

The way we deal with our emotions, for instance, was programmed into us by our conditioning in the first six years of life. In general, emotions are not so well valued in our world. They seem frightening. It can seem we are going to lose control if we allow ourselves to feel and express our emotions. They make us vulnerable. However, vulnerability is also what makes us authentic.

We can ask ourselves what we think when we are experiencing sadness or anger or joy. We can also observe ourselves how we react when someone else is experiencing sadness or anger or joy. How we react to other people's emotions is a reflection of what we think about our own emotions. If I am not comfortable with being sad and crying, of course I won't be comfortable with someone else around me being sad and crying. This is going to bring me back to my own discomfort. On the other hand, if I am comfortable with my emotions, I will be comfortable when other people are experiencing their emotions. I can hold the space for me or anyone to experience an emotion.

We have all heard the belief that boys don't cry, boys get angry. Or that girls don't get angry, girls cry. However, this is not true; these are only beliefs—very limiting ones. Emotions have nothing to do with the gender of the person experiencing them—that is, until that person becomes conditioned by the world.

If my conditioning did not teach me to value my emotions, all I can do is have compassion for them. Obviously, they themselves did not learn to value their emotions, as their conditioning did not teach them to value their emotions. We can go back in time indefinitely. We cannot teach something we were not taught. This is not an opportunity to blame our conditioning. This is a chance to practice compassion. This is an occasion to take responsibility. This is a perfect time to remember Maya Angelou's wise words: "I did then what I knew how to do. Now that I know better, I do better."

This applies to us and to everyone. I did the best I could with what I knew then. Now that I know better, I do better. My family, my culture, and society did the best it could with what it knew. We always do the best we can with our current level of understanding, knowledge, and awareness.

My programming is responsible for making me who I am today. I am responsible for who I become. I am not a baby or child anymore. Now I can take responsibility for what has been programmed into me. It allowed me to survive up to this day. I am grateful. It certainly kept me safe. I have free will. I can choose to reprogram myself with something else if my previous programming is limiting and not to my liking today.

Let Emotions Flow

Emotions are life in us. They flow through us. When we observe a baby, we can see that child experiencing a rainbow of emotions in a very short amount of time. One minute, he or she is so angry. The next minute, he or she is so sad. The next minute, he or she is overjoyed. That baby is alive!

This is how we were before we were conditioned out of this natural way of being. Our families, our cultures, and society teach us that emotions are not allowed. But if we observe wise people, monks, or shamans, we see them expressing their emotions freely—just like a child.

While I was on a plane in 2017, I was watching a beautiful Walt Disney movie called *Moana*. One minute I was laughing wholeheartedly, as some parts of the film are hilarious. The next minute I was crying because I was so touched by the beauty or drama in the film. The next minute, I felt angry by the unfairness I saw in the story. I chose to disregard people around me in the plane. Instead, I chose to tune in to life in me and gave myself permission to express that life. I am alive!

Emotions are energy in motion, just as the name implies: e-motion— not good, not bad, just energy. All emotions just pass through us if allowed to do so. An emotion lasts about ninety seconds, which is the time it takes for the hormones released by the endocrine system to wash through the body and leave. If not allowed to go through the body and be expressed, the emotion will become stored in the body. Then the body will start to live in the past. You will become the emotion, and the emotion will become your identity.

For example, an event happens that makes you sad. If you don't allow yourself to feel and express that sadness, if you don't allow yourself to cry, you can eventually become sadness. Now you don't feel sad; you are sadness. Allowing your emotions to flow through you is an act of self-love. Allowing life in you is loving yourself unconditionally.

Messengers

Emotions are so precious. All emotions are messengers or guides. They are gifts. They are a feedback mechanism. They tell us about us. An emotion tells us what kind of thoughts we are thinking and can make us discover some hidden beliefs we hold.

Developing the ability to listen to and express our emotions can become a valuable strength. Emotions help us navigate the journey of life. They guide us is the direction we are going. It is so empowering to know that they serve a purpose. They carry a message and keep us in touch with our needs. We have all kinds of needs, which fall under physical, emotional, and spiritual needs. To be healthy is to take responsibility for our needs and fulfill them.

We can welcome all our emotions and allow them to move through us by feeling and expressing them. We have the power to allow our emotions to flow through us. If emotions linger, we can help them on their way so they don't become stored in the body and become identities. This would lower our vibration.

CHAPTER 8

Powerful Mind

The Mind Is Everything. What You Think You Become.
—Buddha

The Iceberg Metaphor

Overview

The iceberg represents the mind. It is a great metaphor for our mind that is used by Dr. Sigmund Freud, neurologist and psychoanalyst, and Dr. Carl Gustav Jung, psychiatrist and psychoanalyst.

The visible part of the iceberg is the conscious mind, which is the surface, outer life. The conscious mind is the ego—the personality. It is the logical, reasoning, analytical, and rational mind. The personality is a fundamental part of a person that can relate with the external world. It is also the part that wants to control everything and everyone. A person needs a strong and flexible personality to live a healthy life, to grow, and to evolve. A person needs a strong and flexible conscious mind to interact with the unconscious mind. A person needs an ego but is not the ego.

The submerged part of the iceberg is the unconscious mind, which is the deep inner life. All memories and experiences create beliefs, habits, behaviors, and perceptions, which all reside in the unconscious mind. Most of the mind, 95 percent of it, is unconscious, and it governs most of a person's life.

The wise part of a person resides in the unconscious mind, which is part of Infinite Intelligence or the great mind or the universe. Each person is connected to Infinite Intelligence through intuition. In the unconscious mind, a person has access to the energy, information, and inspiration from the wisdom of the ages, my teacher Nicolas Bornemisza, a Jungian expert, explains in his book *Guérir grâce à nos images intérieures*. Robert A. Johnson, a Jungian analyst, in his book *Inner Work,* writes: "If we try to ignore the inner world, as most of us do, the unconscious will try to find its way into our lives through pathology: our psychosomatic symptoms, compulsions, depressions, and neurosis."[7]

Between the conscious mind and the unconscious mind, the subconscious mind is found. It serves as a buffer zone between the more surface conscious mind and the deeper unconscious part of the mind. In the unconscious mind, you find the collective unconscious. It links every one of us, and in that way, we are all connected. It is also our access to the past, present, and future. "The distinction between past, present, and future is only a stubbornly persistent illusion," said Albert Einstein.

The important thing to understand is that there are many parts to the mind, and we need all of them. The conscious, the subconscious, the unconscious, the collective unconscious, and the great mind are all one. We can also recognize that all these minds, and everyone's mind, are connected with one another and united as *one* mind.

To simplify, let us view the mind as being made up of two parts: the conscious mind and the unconscious mind. When we are in balance, these minds communicate with one another and are in harmony. For example, the unconscious mind, through intuition, can speak to the conscious mind during the day. We can also receive messages in night dreams from the unconscious mind. Also, the unconscious mind hears what we consciously tell ourselves during the day.

There is no separation between these minds. The conscious and unconscious have a two-way communication. When a person starts changing the conscious mind, the change will be communicated to the unconscious mind. When a person starts changing the unconscious mind, the change will be communicated to the conscious mind.

I was trapped in my conscious mind—my ego. This is where my problem resided. I had no idea that a whole world existed outside the prison of my conscious mind. I did not know that I had an inner life and that I am governed by my unconscious mind. MS invited me to open myself to the vast world in me and all around me—to set myself free from the prison of my conscious mind and discover my inner world. What a gift!

Part A: Conscious Mind

My Old Usual Negative Self-Talk

I used to have no awareness of my mental activity. But just as we breathe, we think. We never stop thinking. Mental activity happens on its own, like breathing or digestion or the beat of the heart. It is always happening without our conscious participation. We never stop these activities as long as we are alive.

I had a consistent negative self-talk. I would mentally complain about anything and everything. I would judge myself, others, and situations. I used to be completely trapped in my negative thinking.

When I was working for an actuarial firm, a colleague at work had even given me the nickname grumpy. This gives you an idea of how consistently I was in a bad mood. It was my identity. I was a bad mood.

A Stroke of Insight

In 2008 I came across a beautiful book by Dr. Jill Bolte Taylor titled *My Stroke of Insight: A Brain Scientist's Personal Journey*. This amazing woman was brought to my awareness through Oprah's Super Soul Series. I love listening to this soulful series.

Dr. Taylor is a neuroanatomist. She studied and researched the brain before she had her own brain disorder. One day, she suffered a stroke in the left hemisphere of her brain, and the right side of her body became paralyzed. She was not able to walk, talk, read, write, understand language, or recall any memory of her life. She lost all mental chatter as a result. She had found nirvana! She completely recovered and shared her amazing story.

The left hemisphere of the brain is linear. It deals with details and is concerned about the past and the future. It is the center of language and the source of the voice in our heads. It is where we derive our sense of identity and where we can think, *I am*. It is what keeps us separate from everyone and everything.

The right hemisphere of the brain thinks in pictures. It lives in the present moment and can perceive that everything is energy. It can perceive that we are all one and all united as brothers and sisters. We all have access to nirvana through the right hemisphere.

Both hemispheres are very different from one another. They are separated by the corpus callosum through which they communicate with one another. With the left hemisphere, a person can choose to be a separate ego. Or, a person can choose, with the right hemisphere, to be the life force power of the universe connected to all. We can each choose.

This made me realize that my understanding of the famous saying by the mathematician and philosopher René Descartes, "I think, therefore I am," turns out to be only part of the truth. Dr. Taylor stopped thinking for some time because of the stoke, but she never ceased to exist. Her book helped me on my long journey of realizing that my thinking is the result of a brain function and not who I am.

The Voice in My Head

I came across another amazing book, *A New Earth: Awakening to Your Life's Purpose* by Eckhart Tolle. In 2008 Oprah chose this book for her book club and was very enthusiastic about it.

I completely identified with the voice in my head. I had not been aware I had a voice in my head. I was totally unconscious. I thought the voice in my head was me. Tolle says: "What a liberation to realize that the 'voice in my head' is not who I am. Who am I then? The one who sees that." This book changed my life.

Tolle clearly explains we are not the voices in our heads. We are the awareness behind those voices. What a revelation! Very gradually, I became more aware of that voice. I became the observer of that voice. Slowly, I began to develop some distance between the thoughts in my mind and the observer of those thoughts. I started to lose my identification with that voice. What a relief!

The Only Thing I Can Control

The only thing I can control is my thinking. However, this is not easy, and in fact, this is the hardest thing I can ever do. It is my lifelong learning journey.

In his book, *The Science of Getting Rich*, Wallace D. Wattles writes: "*To think what you want to think is to think TRUTH, regardless of appearances.* Every man has the natural and inherent power to think what he wants to think, but it requires far more effort to do so than it does to think the thoughts which are suggested by appearances. To think according to appearance is easy; to think truth regardless of appearances is laborious, and requires the expenditure of more power than any other work man is called upon to perform."[8]

It is so hard because we naturally think according to the emotions stored in our bodies. Emotions are the result of experiences. We are addicted to the emotions we memorized from different experiences. It helps us tremendously to control our thinking if we liberate these suppressed emotions that are keeping us stuck in the past.

In his book *Breaking the Habit of Being Yourself,* Dr. Dispenza writes: "Warning: when feelings become the means of thinking, or if we cannot think greater than how we feel, we can never change. *To change is to think greater than how we feel.* To change is to act greater than the familiar feelings of the memorized self."[9] He further explains: "In this moment, it seems impossible to think greater than how you feel—and that's why it's so hard to change."[10] The greatest addiction I can ever break is the addiction of being myself.

First, I become aware of my thoughts. I notice the thoughts passing through my mind. I learn that I am not those thoughts. Meditation is my greatest tool. I learn to control my conscious thoughts. I can choose to entertain only thoughts that make me feel good instead of thoughts that make me feel bad. When I take control of my conscious mind, my subconscious mind hears that I have taken control and starts believing what I tell myself.

I learned with teachers like Dr. Kabat-Zinn and so many others that we do not have to believe all of our thoughts. We can choose with our free will which thoughts to entertain and which thoughts to release. We can choose to simply observe our thoughts and let them pass through our minds like clouds moving through the sky. We don't have to cling to them or be caught up by them.

I am fascinated by the incredible number of times I had to hear the same principle over and over and over again so it could begin to sink into my awareness. I heard the same message of "I am not my thoughts" and "I can control my thinking" so many times from so many different teachers.

An amazing amount of study and practice allowed me to finally start believing that thoughts become things when I feel them. Yogi Bhajan was so accurate when he said: "We live in a state of hypnosis." This state of hypnosis makes it very hard to wake up. It is an ongoing journey for me.

My mind can produce the most beautiful thoughts, and it can produce the most horrifying ones. Most thoughts that I hear are not even mine. They come from the collective unconscious. We live in a sea of thoughts. We can choose to let them pass through us and then return to the space of the present moment.

Some Tools to Control the Conscious Mind

We have absolute control over one thing: our conscious thoughts. By controlling our minds, we can also control our bodies and our realities. Our minds cocreate our bodies and our realities. We have an amazing innate ability to cocreate lives we love living that are in harmony with the purpose of our souls.

Nothing matters more than what we are thinking. We can control what we are thinking in this moment. What we are thinking governs how we are feeling. So, more precisely, nothing matters more than how we are feeling in this moment. It is important to pay attention to how we are feeling. Here are four tools to help control the conscious mind.

Tool 1: Notice What You Are Noticing

With your awareness, you can notice what you are noticing. This is the first brave thinking tool Mary Morrissey teaches:

Can you notice your left hand?
Can you notice your right foot?
Can you notice the tip of your nose?
Can you notice the gentle breeze on your skin?
Can you notice the smell in the air around you?
Can you notice the sounds in your environment?
Can you notice your thoughts?
Can you notice your feelings and emotions?

You notice with the infinite side of yourself, the observer in you.

Every moment you are thinking. Thinking never stops. It is important to notice your thoughts and choose empowering ones, such as thoughts on gratitude, love, peace, and joy.

When you wake up in the morning, what are you thinking?
When you brush your teeth, take a shower, and get dressed, what are you thinking?
When you are going about your day and accomplishing any mundane task, what are you thinking?
When you are doing the dishes or the laundry, when you are walking or driving or using public transportation, what are you thinking?
When you are doing physical exercise, what are you thinking?
When you are talking or listening to someone or something, what are you thinking?
When you are falling asleep at night, what are you thinking?

Every moment is an opportunity to notice what is going on in your mind. You don't have to be sitting in a formal meditation practice to be aware of your mind. You can be aware of it at any moment. You are always thinking. Every moment is an opportunity to notice your thoughts and choose what you want to think.

Tool 2: Repeat a Mantra

You can choose to repeat a mantra. A mantra is a tool for your mind. It has a highly positive vibration. It has the power to transform your mind. It can help you focus on something positive. There are innumerable mantras from which you can choose.

Sat Nam is a classic kundalini yoga mantra that I love. *Sat* means "truth," and *Nam* means "identity." It literally means "truth is my identity." You can repeat *Sat* on the inhale and *Nam* on the exhale. Thus, synchronizing the mental, or verbal, repetition of the mantra with your breathing. This adds even more power to this practice. You can also repeat the universal mantra *om*. It is believed to be the sound of the universe.

While I was attending the kripalu yoga teacher training course in 2010, my intuition spoke to me very clearly through a synchronicity in my environment. I did not hear the message at first. We were studying the first two chapters of the yoga sutras of Patanjali. There are fifty-one sutras in chapter 1 and fifty-five sutras in chapter 2. *Sutra* means "rule" in Sanskrit.

Our teacher had each of us draw two numbers for the sutras we were to study and then asked each of us to explain to the rest of the group. Even though this drawing looked random, he informed us that it was not. Each of us would get exactly the sutras best suited to our needs.

I did not know at the time that the universe is perfect and that all is in divine order. I did not know there are no random events, no coincidences, and no mistakes in this universe and that life unfolds with mathematical precision. As a result, I did not hear my teacher's wisdom.

I studied no fewer than five versions of this book. I really wanted to understand the sutras that I had drawn and to be able to explain them to my classmates. I drew sutras 1-29 and 1-30.

Sutra 1–29 goes like this: "Hence comes knowledge of the Atman and destruction of the obstacles to that knowledge."[11]

This means that from the repetition of the mantra *om* comes the knowledge of our souls and the destruction of the obstacles to knowing our souls. This sutra recognizes the power of our words, for better or for worse. This power has been known throughout the ages.

This sutra reminds us that we are mainly in a state of reverie or trance. We are always repeating words in our minds. Usually, we are not aware of our constant mental activity and do nothing to control it. Because we are mostly unconscious, our mental activity is primarily dictated by the external world: situations, conditions, and circumstances.

This sutra advises us to replace our thoughts with the mantra *om*. This will gradually allow for greater control of our thoughts. This will develop our ability to concentrate and turn our attention inward. This will turn our awareness toward our souls—our real selves. This will destroy the obstacle to knowing our real selves.

Sutra 1–30 goes like this: "Sickness, mental laziness, doubt, lack of enthusiasm, sloth, craving for sense pleasure, false perception, despair caused by failure to concentrate, and unsteadiness in concentration: these distractions are the obstacles to knowledge."[12]

While sutra 1–30 gives us the list of the distractions, sutra 1–29 tells us how to destroy those obstacles of distraction. Keeping our attention focused on the universal mantra *om*, and giving it meaning, leads us to knowing our real selves. It helps us to overcome all the distractions to getting to know our true selves.

Of all the sutras, I drew the only one talking about sickness—what a coincidence. I did not find this coincidence particularly interesting in that moment. How could I? I was still in profound denial that I was sick, and I did not think overcoming MS was possible.

I did not think I could have anything to do with what was happening in my mind, let alone my body. This experience guided me a little further on my journey to realizing the power of my thoughts. Also, I did not know about my real self—my soul. I knew only about my ego.

Tool 3: Repeat an Affirmation

You can choose to repeat an affirmation to yourself. There exists an infinite variety from which to choose. Louise Hay, the queen of affirmations, has created beautiful ones. In her book *You Can Heal Your Life*, she lists diseases or physical problems and the corresponding affirmation to support healing. I love the one she suggests for multiple sclerosis: "I am safe and free."[13] It really resonates with me and makes total sense.

A sense of safety was certainly lacking for me. I had no idea I am a spiritual being having a human experience. I was trapped in my left brain. Getting to know I am never alone as a spiritual being certainly developed a sense of safety in me. I am more than my reason—I also have the gift of intuition, which connects me to Infinite Intelligence. This is not intellectual knowledge. This is something I came to realize and experience because I am now open to the world in me and around me.

I think a sense of safety is lacking when someone is diagnosed with MS. A sense of safety is developed in experiencing inherent connection with Infinite Intelligence through the soul. Baron-Reid explains this beautifully in her book *Uncharted: The Journey Through Uncertainty to Infinite Possibility.*

A sense of freedom was also lacking for me. I thought I had to be like everybody else. It feels so liberating and freeing to be me. I did not know that my privilege in this lifetime is to be the unique individual that I am. "The privilege of a lifetime is being who you are," Joseph Campbell says. We all have that privilege if we dare to own it. The world would be so much richer if all people expressed their unique gifts. I don't imitate my parents or anyone else, but I don't reject them either—I am simply me.

I think a sense of freedom is also lacking when a person is diagnosed with MS. I came to understand that MS can happen when you forget your own path and follow your family's path. You can become lost trying to live your parents' lives instead of living your own life and following your own calling. Dr. Oliver Soulier explains this in detail in his DVD *Sortir de la sclérose en plaques*, which means, "coming out of multiple sclerosis." The way out of MS is following your own path by becoming the unique individual you were meant to be. This is the goal of the individuation process.

Tool 4: Focus on a Vision

You can focus your thoughts on a vision of a life you would love to live. You can focus on your dreams and what you want to manifest. Anything that makes you feel good. It is your mind. You can choose which thought seeds you want to plant in your mind now to enjoy its fruits later.

Having a vision for your life gives your mind a direction. It allows you to take control of your mind, instead of your mind controlling you, and leads you to live "a vision driven life, instead of a condition driven life," as Mary Morrissey teaches.

The way to create is to hold in your mind a vision of a life you would love living that honors your longings and discontents. Asking yourself what you would love puts you in harmony with your soul's purpose. Listen to what is seeking to emerge through you. Test your dream by asking yourself these questions to find out if it is worthy of your time and energy:

1. Would I feel more *alive?*
2. Is it in alignment with my *core values?*
3. Does it require that I *grow?*
4. Do I need help from a *higher power?*
5. Does it have *good* in it for *others?*

You need to answer *yes* to all five questions. I learned these essential questions during my training to become a transformational life coach with Mary Morrissey.

Feel the emotions you would feel if it were real in time and space now. Take consistent and repeated actions in the direction of those dreams. This is a process; it is not easy and takes practice, repetition, and support. Put how it will happen on hold and surrender to allow the universe to guide you to inspired actions.

As long as you are breathing, you are cocreating with life. Holding a vision in your mind that is in harmony with your soul's purpose is the way to create a life by design instead of by default. I became a transformational life coach to help people create lives they love living from the inside out. Transformation is my passion.

Part B: Unconscious Mind

Foundation

My understanding is that the unconscious mind is part of Infinite Intelligence. I came to understand and believe that Infinite Intelligence, life, God, love, spirit, universal intelligence, the great mind, cosmic consciousness, the matrix of the universe, source, the quantum field, a higher power, our essence, and our life force are all the same. In her book *Uncharted: The Journey Through Uncertainty to Infinite Possibility*, Baron-Reid helped me reach that understanding. Books by Nicolas Bornemisza and Robert A. Johnson on the unconscious mind also guided me in that direction and informed me that Jung likens the unconscious mind to God.

The beauty of this powerful and loving unconscious mind is that it is always trying to help us and heal us. Its goal is to make us whole by resolving the unconscious conflicts and opposites in us as we become more and more conscious. Its other goal is to free us from all the conditioning we received so we can become our unique selves. It really is the wise part of us.

There are many ways to access the unconscious mind. You can use your body like I first did. (See chapter 6.) You can use your conscious mind to influence your unconscious mind as you become more and more conscious of your unconscious self. (See chapter 8, part A.) You can interpret your night dreams and pay attention to the synchronicities in our life. (See chapter 8, part B.) You can use writing to transform a limiting belief into an expansive affirmation. (See chapter 8, part C.) You can use meditation to lower your brain-wave frequencies to get into the operating system that is your unconscious mind. (See chapter 8, part D.) I know there are more ways.

Night Dreams

In my late teens, I started dreaming of tigers regularly. For many years, there would be tigers in my dreams. They were just there, bringing their powerful and peaceful presence. It was very intense, but I never paid any attention to these dreams and never looked up the symbolic meaning of tigers. I was so rational that dreams and symbols were not a part of my world, even though dreams are very prevalent in my sleep.

One day when I was in my late twenties, the whole left side of my body became paralyzed, seemingly out of the blue. Eventually, I wondered: why my left side? I began to become interested in the symbolic life. The left side of the body is symbolic of the feminine side.

When I started studying the unconscious mind as part of my healing journey, I learned that tigers are the supreme symbol of femininity. Femininity was the part of myself that I denied. Anything feminine,

I did not want to hear—that is, femininity in a yin sense in yin-yang model. I began to learn about and integrate the yin side of me and life (more about that in chapter 10). I learned that it is worth listening to my dreams as they have meaning and are really trying to help me.

The unconscious mind tries to communicate with the conscious mind during the day and during the night. It is constantly trying to inspire us, inform us, and guide us through synchronistic events during the day and dreams at night. We need to forever develop and deepen our listening skills. It is important that we learn to listen to life's gentle messages. The more we listen, the better we become at listening.

Life is always talking to us and conspiring for our greatest good. We can begin by recognizing that life is intelligent and loving. We can start by acknowledging that there is an inner wise self in the unconscious mind. We have an inner reliable friend, as my Jungian analyst Nicolas Bornemisza calls it, after having analyzed more than thirty-five thousand dreams.

If you really want to receive the help your unconscious mind so lovingly offers at all times, you can decide to be open to learn its symbolic language. My analyst calls it poetically the language of the soul. Symbols come during the day and during the night. At first, it may feel like learning Chinese. It is an ongoing process. You can learn if you become curious and you keep an open heart and mind to the meaning of all these symbols surrounding us. A good book to interpret symbols is a great place to start.

The following French books were recommended to me:
- *Dictionnaire des symboles: Mythes, rêves, coutumes, gestes, formes, figures, couleurs, nombres* by Jean Chevalier and Alain Gheerbrant

- *La Symbologie des rêves: Le Corps humain* by Jacques De La Rocheterie
- *La Symbologie des rêves: La nature* by Jacques De La Rocheterie

Every person typically receives five or six dreams every night. There are many different types of dreams. A dream could answer a question that you ask your unconscious mind before you go to sleep. A dream could be a way of soothing a desire or to compensate a conscious attitude. A dream could be a premonition, a warning, or a nightmare informing you of something in your attitude toward life that is inappropriate. A dream could reassure or console you. A dream could also belong to the collective unconscious and not concern you personally.

More often than not, your dream is informing you about you. It is always for your greatest good. Every dream is beautiful and positive. You can decide to move past your judgment toward it. It is good to make a ritual in your waking hours to symbolize the meaning of your dreams. This informs your unconscious mind that you received the message. It can be any physical action that symbolizes the message. It can be a simple walk around the block.

Sometimes I find the message is obvious. However, most of the time I find it is less obvious. But I am always curious, and I always keep an open heart and mind. I ask my unconscious mind for clarity and express my genuine interest in understanding the message. It becomes easier with interest, practice, and knowledge. I can use my intuition and ask for help.

We can decide to pay attention to the symbols coming into our lives. When we dream, we can ask ourselves how we feel regarding the symbols. Symbols that are not understood become symptoms. This is all loving and for our greatest good. The messages are important for us to understand. Once we get the messages, we will have become wiser and happier versions of ourselves. Understanding symbols opens us to the energy of the universe and allows us to be inspired, to heal, and to transform.

On the following page is a very brief list of some of the most common symbols we can encounter in our dreams with a very basic and general meaning. This is just a very tiny glimpse in a word or two. Keep in mind that the definition of a symbol can take multiple pages in a dictionary. Symbols can have two opposite definitions and require personal associations to be fully understood. This comes from this French online course from my teachers Marie Lise Labonté and Nicolas Bornemisza: https://vimeo.com/121374415.

Symbols and Their Meanings

Symbol	Meaning
ocean, sea	collective unconscious
river	flow of life
pool	our unconscious
water leak, seepage, puddle	emotions
Earth	Mother Earth, feminine
mountain	elevation
animals	our animal instincts
cat, horse	domesticated instincts
cat	selfish, sensual
all felines	femininity
lion	masculine royal energy, collective
house	body, psychic structure
kitchen	transformation
basement	unconscious
window	vision to see the outside world
car	evolution
plane	elevation

Synchronicity

A synchronicity is the way the unconscious mind speaks to the conscious mind during the day. Just like stars in the sky are still there during the day, dreams happen during the day. They are called synchronicities by Jung. A synchronicity is what makes oracles true. An oracle can be the tarot or the I Ching.

Jung defines a synchronicity as a significant coincidence between an event in the inside and an event on the outside that don't seem to be related in a cause and effect manner. The most obvious synchronicity is a disease, but not all diseases are synchronicities. A synchronicity is something happening in the soul that manifests in the body or in life.

MS was a synchronicity in my life. Many things were happening inside me—in my soul. I was not even aware I had an inside life or that I was a soul. MS was a huge wake-up call. MS woke me up and ultimately led to my healing.

A synchronicity could be a diagnosis, a depression, an accident, or a financial crisis. It could be a separation, a divorce, or the death of a loved one. It can be anything we did not expect and cannot control. It can be positive, like the unforeseen meeting of someone or a book that falls from the shelf at the perfect moment.

Let's say you lose your wallet during the day. Knowing that life is filled with loving intelligence, you can become curious about the meaning of this event. You can ask yourself: what does a wallet represent to me? It could represent your identity. Could this event mean you are losing your identity and need to find a new one? Only you know for sure—become curious. Ask your unconscious mind to be guided to the meaning of this event and remain open.

In 2011 I lost my wallet. I did not see any meaning in that event at the time. Looking back, I can see that life was guiding me to find a new identity. It was time for me to let go of my old identity of being an actuary and discover a new one.

The Shadow

Another important thing I learned is we all have a shadow part of ourselves. This is where our richness and uniqueness reside. In our night dreams, it is mostly represented by a person of the same sex as the dreamer. So, if I dream of another woman, she represents one unconscious aspect of myself.

The shadow is defined as the unlived life. She could be a part of me I repressed and never made part of my conscious life. She could also be a part of me I don't express and have not yet discovered, like a talent or a skill. The shadow is always seen reflected in another person. The defects or qualities I do not see in myself, I will see in another person.

The goal is to recognize this unconscious part of myself and try to make her a part of my conscious life. I do not want to give her dominion over my life or ignore her. I want to find a common ground so we can both exist. I want to negotiate with her and bring into my life the qualities she embodies. I can develop these qualities in myself, or I can befriend someone with these qualities.

My teacher gave us a great example to understand the shadow. "Let's say you are a communist. Your shadow would be a capitalist," Nicolas Bornemisza says. We need to be careful of any extreme position we assume. Unconsciously, we assume the opposite extreme.

Anima/Animus

In our night dreams, we can also dream of a person of the opposite sex. Jung coined the term *animus* for the man in a woman's dreams and the term *anima* for the woman in a man's dreams. As a woman, when I dream of a man, I may acquire information on my inner masculinity. When a man dreams of a woman, he may gain knowledge on his inner femininity.

This can inform us of our inner couple, which is the feminine side and the masculine side. We all have this inner couple, and the goal is to have a harmonious inner couple. This inner relationship will change and evolve over your lifetime. It can be tumultuous in the beginning. The person of the opposite sex could eventually become a guide for you.

The Self

The self represents inner totality, according to Jung. The self is inner wholeness, of which we are only partially aware. Realizing the self is the never-ending journey of aligning the conscious mind with the unconscious mind.

First, you make the unconscious conscious by gradually integrating your shadow and your anima/animus. Second, you set yourself free from conditioning by becoming the unique individual you are meant to be. This is the lifetime work of individuation.

In a night dream, the self can be represented as an old, wise man or woman. It can be a baby or a child. It can be a president, a cleaner, a trickster, a politician, or a revered artist. It can be a religious authority such as Christ. It can be anything that seems positive to us or even dangerous.

The self can be represented by a circle, a square, a mandala, or the number four. It can be symbolized by a crystal, a gemstone, or an extraordinary animal such as a black cow with dots. Or it can be a symbol reuniting and harmonizing opposites such as a black-and-white floor, a moon and a sun, or a hermaphrodite.

Individuation

Individuation is a term coined by Jung. It is the process of realizing the self. The unconscious mind—life—guides you. Life invites you toward the road less traveled to embrace your individuality. The best way to love yourself is to be yourself. Only you can express life in your own unique way and the unique gifts you have to offer.

I received an invitation with my diagnosis of MS. I am learning a whole new way of being. I was invited to connect with my life force and with my instincts. I was invited to connect with my power to choose and to act. I was invited to connect with my heart, my soul, and my intuition. I was invited to dare to think for myself and to be myself. I was invited to connect with the spiritual side of my being. I was invited to grow up.

I was invited on the road less traveled. It is not the well-worn path—it is the unknown. I listen to my intuition to travel this path. I develop a relationship with my own inner wisdom. I realize I am the master of my life and the highest authority in my life.

I aim to be flexible with whatever comes my way, to go with the flow of life, and to follow its current. I aim to act and not react but respond. I aim to live and not only survive but thrive.

The process of individuation is likened to the hero's journey described by the mythologist Joseph Campbell in his book *The Hero with a Thousand Faces*. It is a dark night of the soul. We all have to go through dark nights of the soul to birth better versions of ourselves. The hero's journey is, in truth, the human's journey, and it is described in three phases.

The first phase is the departure.

The departure is the call to adventure. A crisis forces us to question ourselves and our lives. The call to adventure forces us out of the lives we know. The departure could be forced by some challenge life brings to our doorsteps. It could be a diagnosis, an accident, a depression, a heartbreak, or the meeting of someone. We can refuse this call to adventure because we have free will. We can resist life. The easy choice would be to accept the call to adventure. The less resistance, the easier the journey.

I received this call. When I was first diagnosed with MS, I denied it as much as I could. Every fiber of my being resisted it. I refused to go on an adventure—life's adventure. I wanted to remain in the well-known territory of the familiar. But my disease became worse. I got to a point where denial was not an option. I was sick. I was really sick.

Denial is understandable. The known is comfortable. The unknown seems frightening just because it is unknown. It is uncomfortable to leave the familiar. It is not popular, and it takes effort—that is, until the comfortable familiar becomes uncomfortable. When the pain becomes bigger than the gain, we change. This is when I decided to move out of the familiar and change.

This call to adventure is nature's response to someone's call for individuation, whether conscious or unconscious. I remember at the end of my kundalini yoga teacher training course I had asked life to help me find a deeper meaning to life. When this diagnosis came, it never crossed my mind that it could be a response to my calling for more. It took me many years to open up to this possibility.

It was a painful journey that I would not wish on my worst enemy. But the gift it has given me I wish on everyone.

The call to adventure invites us to change and become our authentic selves. It points us in the direction of our own growth and invites us to evolve. This call to adventure is an invitation to get out of the prison of comfort and conformity where we are trapped. This is exactly the goal of the individuation process.

This departure could also be chosen. We could receive an intuition or experience a vision or dream that it is time to change, to grow, and to get out of our comfort zones.

The second phase is the initiation.

This is the time for challenges and realizations. This is the time to do the work required to change, to evolve, and to outgrow our limits. This is the time to become who we are capable of becoming and free ourselves from parental conditioning.

I was blessed to find amazing mentors on my path who helped me become a whole new person—my authentic self. I released tensions, suppressed emotions, and limiting beliefs—I raised my vibration. I gave meaning to what was happening.

The third phase is the return.

I came back from life's adventure with a power I never knew existed. I came back with an ability to travel between two worlds: the conscious and the unconscious. I came back knowing I am a soul having a human experience, always connected to Infinite Intelligence.

I came back with a willingness to listen to life. I came back knowing that I can act with confidence with life as my greatest ally. I came back knowing the universe has my back. I came back knowing I am more than any situation, circumstance, or condition.

I now have a different awareness in my day-to-day life. I realize that in an infinite universe I am never alone. I discovered I am always guided by life from birth to death.

Part C: Body and Mind Are *One*

Such a Revelation!

My healing journey really made me experience the fact that body and mind are one. For me, mind and body had always been separate. Over here was my mind, and over there was my body— two separate entities having nothing to do with one another. I learned this fact first intellectually during my kundalini yoga teacher training course. I learned that mind, emotions, and body are one: they only have different forms.

It was Einstein who first proved this fact with his famous equation $E = mc^2$. Energy and matter are one and the same, which is a well-known and recognized fact today. There are countless books on the subject, and Harvard even has a mind/body department. I had the chance of experiencing this truth during my holistic bodywork training. You can easily experience it for yourself.

You can close your eyes and in your mind play a sexual fantasy. Imagine all the vivid details, and in no time, your body will become physically aroused. All the responses in your body come from thoughts in your mind. A mental sexual fantasy will immediately show you how body and mind are connected.

Or the next time you are feeling down, you can pick your favorite song and start dancing your heart out. Pretty quickly, you will find yourself in an elevated and happier state of mind. Physical movements will immediately show you how mind and body are connected.

Change the Body, Change the Mind

The bodywork I practiced intensively for more than two years really changed my body. It liberated my body by releasing physical tensions and suppressed emotions. It allowed me to reunite with my body that was stuck in the past.

At first, my body felt like it was a concrete cylinder. I had been living trapped in my body, feeling separate from life in me and all around me. Practicing the body movements made this cylinder gently and slowly crack open and tumble down. They released me from the prison of my body and opened me up to life.

After some time, I noticed that my mind was changing too from working on my body. How could that be? I had always believed that my mind and my body were separate and had nothing to do with one another.

As my body was relaxing and opening to life, my mind was also relaxing and opening to life. By releasing the tensions from my body, my mind was also releasing its tensions. Week after week, month after month, my mind was changing as my body was changing. I experienced that body and mind are one. I experienced that by changing my body, I can change my mind. I was amazed.

Change the Mind, Change the Body

We can also change our bodies by changing our minds. I worked at transforming some limiting beliefs during my holistic bodywork training. I experienced once again that mind and body are one. I continued to be amazed.

While using writing to transform a belief, I could feel my body transforming as my mind was transforming. As I was transforming one of my limiting beliefs on love, I could feel the muscles in the deepest layer of my back relaxing more deeply. It was happening in real time.

During my training, I learned a technique to transform a limiting belief based on neurolinguistic programming (NLP). I explored some deep beliefs that I had around love and around life, for example. I began to ask myself what my beliefs were on those subjects. If those beliefs were limiting and not empowering, I practiced a written technique to transform a limiting belief into an expansive affirmation.

The point to remember is that through the written repetition of an expansive affirmation, we can change a limiting belief in our unconscious mind. Because mind and body are one, changing the mind changes the body.

The key to changing the unconscious mind is repetition, repetition, repetition. Connecting that repetition with an elevated emotion changes the unconscious mind. To change a belief, we have to think the opposite thought again and again and again and become emotionally involved.

The old belief will die for lack of nourishment if it's not fed. R. Buckminster Fuller tells us: "You never change things by fighting the existing reality. To change something, build a new model that makes the existing model obsolete."

Technique to Transform a Limiting Belief into an Expansive Affirmation

1. Inquire about your limiting belief.

- For example, ask yourself: what do I believe about love or life?
- Do not censor yourself. Write down everything that comes to mind.
- Do this for at least fifteen minutes and then pick the most limiting belief.

For example, I had the limiting belief that love is weak.

2. Transform that limiting belief into an expansive affirmation that will resolve the limiting belief.

    - Use only positive words.
    - Avoid words like *I believe, I must, I think,* and *I want.*
    - Use words like *I allow, I get used to, I choose, I accept, I give myself permission,* and *I recognize.*
    - Use short sentences.
    - Do not involve others or a condition.
    - Start the affirmation with *me* followed by your name.
    - Write in the present tense.

    I transformed my limiting belief into: Me, Mounina, I choose the power of love.

3. Once you've found your expansive affirmation, take a sheet of paper and divide it into two columns and do the following process:

    - In the left column, begin by writing your expansive affirmation.
    - In the right column, write any response your unconscious mind might have to your expansive affirmation.
    - Come back to the left column and write your expansive affirmation again.

- Go back to the right column and write any response your unconscious mind might have to your expansive affirmation. It could be a memory, a physical sensation in your body, an emotion (express it), a voice (from a parent, for instance), another belief, or nothing at all.
- If you get the same limiting belief three times as a response in the right column, it means you found a deeper belief to transform.
- Do this for at least forty-five minutes every day.
- Do this until you see in your day-to-day life or in your body that the belief was transformed.
- To end, write your expansive affirmation on both sides of the sheet.
- Now burn the sheet as you are taking the waste out. You do not want to reread what you wrote or keep it for later. You want to destroy it.

What Is a Belief?

Beliefs are held in the unconscious mind. A belief is a thought loaded with an emotion. It is a thought we keep repeating to ourselves. Most of our beliefs come from our conditioning, and we form most of them in the first years of our lives. A belief is a rational conclusion or judgment that the cerebral cortex draws from an experience. It comes from the left brain. It could be something someone else said or a deduction, an interpretation, or a generalization that we made. It could be something personal or shared by many. It can become an identity to serve as protection from a perceived threat, and it can provide a sense of safety.

Beliefs are arranged in layers. Just as your muscles are organized in layers, so are the beliefs you hold. Once you have released a surface belief, a deeper one will rise up. All of our beliefs form a web, linking everything we believe in. This is similar to the connective tissues in the body, which link every part of the body into one whole.

Beliefs are so strong that they create a person's reality. They are that powerful! They also determine how a person perceives his or her reality and how that reality is interpreted. I want to emphasize the limiting aspect of beliefs. When something is outside a person's beliefs, that person doesn't even see it, and its existence is not even a possibility.

MS is believed to be incurable. This belief is in the collective unconscious. Doctors, specialists, and all MS associations reaffirm this belief. Because the possibility of overcoming MS is not an accepted belief yet, it requires a stretching out of our belief system to accept the fact that it could be otherwise and to undo the voodoo curse this diagnosis represents.

We have beliefs about everything. We have beliefs about life, love, God, reality, time, space, past and future, who we think we are, other people, our families, men and women, the different cultures, education, and politics. We also have beliefs about the different temperaments, age, sleep, weight, beauty, biology, change, happiness, logic, creativity, money, and success.

We need beliefs because this is how we function in life. Beliefs can be expansive or contractive. They can be life giving or not. However, we are not bound by our beliefs. We can decide to change them if they are not empowering. We do not have enough time in life to change all of our limiting beliefs. However, a great deal can be accomplished. What if it were easy?

In his book *Breaking the Habit of Being Yourself*, Dr. Dispenza writes: "True empowerment comes when we start to look deeply at our beliefs. We may find their roots in the conditioning of religion, culture, society, education, family, the media, and even our genes (the latter being imprinted by the sensory experiences of our current lives, as well as untold generations). Then we weigh those old ideas against some new paradigms that may serve us better."[14]

The Mind Is Stronger Than the Body

In his book *Healing and Recovery* and in his map of consciousness, which you can find online, Dr. David R. Hawkins explains the relationship between mind, body, and spirit. It is important to comprehend this relationship for self-healing. He defines this map: "It is an exponential model (to the base 10) that evolved out of a composite of decades of research in a variety of fields. It documents the first time that these energy fields have ever been calibrated."[15]

This map of consciousness measures the relative energy field. The energy fields go from 0 to 1,000. It starts with death, which is calibrated at zero. The energy fields of the body, the earth, and truth begin at 200. Intellect, reason, logic, and what the mind believes begin at 400. The mind is stronger than the body. "The body will do what the mind believes,"[16] he explains. I love to cancel any limiting thought I hear with: I love myself unconditionally now. I am an infinite, powerful, unique, and magnificent being of the universe.

We have to "stand guard at the portal of our mind," as Ralph Waldo Emerson said. We watch closely what the mind believes and cancel any limiting program by saying to ourselves: "I no longer believe in that. I am an infinite being, and I am not subject to that. I am only subject to what I hold in mind,"[17] Dr. Hawkins writes.

The energy field of unconditional love begins at 500. Healing, gratitude, and forgiveness start at 540. Spirit begins at 600. It is where enlightenment begins, which means going beyond duality and identification with the small, personal self—the ego.

Dr. Hawkins explains: "Because the body reflects what the mind believes, and the mind reflects our spiritual position, spirit has the greatest power of all. Therefore, our spiritual position literally determines whether we have a healthy body or not."[18] Spirit over mind over matter.

When we realize that the benefit of being sick is smaller than the pain and suffering of being sick, we can heal. When we realize that we do not need the sense of importance an illness brings because we can derive our sense of importance from the identification with our real selves, we can heal.

Part D: Brain Waves

Meditation on Space

We can access the unconscious mind through meditation. We can work at lowering our brain-wave frequencies from beta to alpha to theta and even delta. We move from the outer world of the conscious mind to the inner word of the unconscious mind. Meditation on space—open focus meditation—as taught by Dr. Dispenza allows us to do so. Please refer to his books: *Breaking the Habit of Being Yourself: How to Lose Your Mind and Create a New One* and *Becoming Supernatural: How Common People Are Doing the Uncommon*, in which Dr. Dispenza explains brain waves in depth and gives these examples.

We can learn to shift our attention from a narrow focus on matter to an open focus on energy or space or nothing—repeated shifting slows down the frequency of our brain waves. We remember, in learning to do so, that reality is 99.99999 percent energy and 0.00001 percent matter. We can learn to sense and feel the energy instead of think of matter—our bodies, our environments (people, places, and things), and time.

We spend most of our waking time in a brain-wave frequency called beta, in the conscious mind, where the outer world appears more real than the inner world. The brain processes data from our five senses and creates meaning and coherence between the inner and outer worlds. We begin to live in beta when we are about twelve years old. We are then only aware of the outer world and are cut away from the inner world. There are three types of beta frequencies.

Low-range beta is 13 to 15 hertz (cycles per seconds), and it is when you are relaxed with nothing threatening happening in the outer world. You are aware of your body in time and space. This could be when you are reading or listening to something or someone interesting.

Medium-range beta is 16 to 22 hertz, and it is when you are more vigilant and have more focused attention on external stimuli. This could be when you are in a group and have to remember everyone's name or are learning. This is good stress, and you are not out of balance.

High-range beta is 22 to 50 hertz, and it is when you are completely overwhelmed by the hormones of stress and have too much focused concentration on matter. You are experiencing a survival emotion, such as "anxiety, depression, frustration, anger, guilt, pain, worry, or sadness."[19] You are in emergency mode. It is meant to be short term and leads to stress and imbalance if experienced long term. It is an incoherent state. High-range beta is more than three times faster than low-range beta and twice as fast as medium-range beta.

When you close your eyes, slow your breathing, and move your attention inward, you lower your brain waves from all the possible variation of beta to alpha, which is 8 to 13 hertz. These are brain-wave frequencies from six to twelve years old, in which the inner world is more real than the outer world, as this is where children place the majority of their attention. When you close your eyes, you naturally begin to move into the alpha brain-wave pattern because 80 percent of sensory information comes from the eyes. You are calmer and more relaxed. You are beyond your analytical mind—you think and analyze less. You have more access to your imagination, you are more creative, and you daydream more. You enter a light meditative state.

In beta brain waves, most of your attention is on the outer world and in the conscious mind. While in alpha brain waves, on the other hand, you place more of your attention on your inner world and begin to enter into the subconscious mind. Alpha brain waves are the bridge between conscious and subconscious.

As you keep practicing and deepening your meditation, you slow down your brain-wave frequency to theta, which is 4 to 8 cycles per second. This is how children are from two to six years old. The body begins falling asleep while the conscious mind is awake and mainly the inner world exists. This is deep meditation where you are half awake and half asleep. You are now deep in your subconscious mind. Because the body is the unconscious mind where programs, habits, and beliefs are stored, when you get into theta brain waves, you have access to reprogram yourself with elevated emotions and empowering beliefs while the body/mind is asleep.

Over time and with advanced practice, you can even get to delta brain waves, which is 0.5 to 4 hertz. These are brain waves from birth to two years old. This state usually comes during deep, restorative sleep.

I am learning to become familiar with my brain waves and to move from beta to alpha to theta and, with persistent work, to delta. I am learning to get passed the analytical mind to enter the subconscious mind toward the unconscious mind. In doing so, I am learning to become pure consciousness as I practice being no body, no one, no thing, no where, in no time. When we fall asleep we naturally move from beta to alpha to theta to delta. We take the reverse road every morning when we wake up and move from delta to theta to alpha to beta. This is why morning and night are good times to meditate as the door to the subconscious naturally opens.

CHAPTER 9

Loving Soul

To the Personality, Judgment is The Natural
Consequence of Suffering. To the Soul, Suffering
is the Natural Consequence of Judgment.
—Robert Schwartz

From Africa to Canada

I was born in Montreal, Canada. At six months old, I moved with my family to the little town of Zouerate in the country of Mauritania in Africa. My dad was born in Mauritania, and he wanted to go back after coming to Canada to study and meeting my mother.

My life in Africa was simple and authentic. I was surrounded by the essence of life—people and nature. I remember being happy and innocent. I had a fascination with the process the caterpillar goes through to become a butterfly. I collected all kinds of beautiful caterpillars and waited in awe as they transformed into magnificent butterflies. I remember feeling connected to something intangible— something I could not see. When I moved from Africa to Canada at ten years old, I lost that connection. I ended up feeling all alone.

It was very traumatic for me to move to a country so different from what I had known. My young ten-year-old mind could not comprehend such an extreme difference. It was in that moment that I retreated into my head and away from my heart. In my head, I could not feel the pain of being so different in a world doing everything possible to make us all the same. But I was also not really alive.

In Mauritania, poverty is all around, but so is richness. People are connected to one another and to something greater. People come from their hearts. They have nothing, yet they are ready to give everything. Most don't have many material possession, yet they have hearts as big as the earth.

In Canada the majority of people are richer. There is safety, drinking water, and food, generally speaking. There is a lot of material abundance available. But on another level, people are poorer. They are poor in their connections with one another and with something greater. They value their minds more than their hearts.

It was in that moment that I disconnected from my soul. People say the soul is the heart or connected to the heart. It was in that moment that I disconnected from my heart and closed my heart. The pain was unbearable. In an attempt to protect myself from the pain I was feeling, I disconnected from my heart, from everyone, and from everything. It was in that moment that I locked myself in my rational mind.

Higher Dimension

In 2010 I completed my kripalu yoga teacher training course. One weekend, our group had to go on a three-day retreat. I suddenly reconnected with my heart, but only briefly. However, I had a glimpse that perhaps I had a heart. It was a wonderful, warm feeling of "I exist, and I matter."

That was a new feeling for me. I did not feel that I existed or that I mattered. At that point, I was very sick. I had been diagnosed with MS after a first crisis in 2007. But I was still in denial of the fact that I was sick. This feeling of self-compassion that came out of the blue felt very soothing. From that moment on, I began opening to the fact that perhaps I am more than meets the eye. I began to think that perhaps this diagnosis was happening for a reason.

In 2014 I was guided to a very particular book titled *Your Soul's Plan: Discovering the Real Meaning of the Life You Planned Before You Were Born* by Robert Schwartz. It conveys the idea that I am a soul and that my soul could have chosen this challenge that came in the form of a diagnosis. My soul could have even made this choice before I was born. But I have free will. It is my choice to decide how I will respond to this condition.

This book conveys the idea that events in our lives happen for a reason. It offers the idea that challenges in our lives are here to show us we are the loves of our lives and love is inside. Difficult situations are here so we can wake up to the fact that we create our own realities with our thoughts, feelings, and actions.

I find this is true. This diagnosis invited me to wake up to the fact that I am more than my personality—I am a soul. It invited me to wake up to the fact that I matter and that I am the love of my life, so I matter indeed. It all starts with me, and everything comes from me.

This might sound egotistical, but it is not. It is actually the opposite. When I realize that love is inside, I don't spend my life looking outside for what is inside. When I realize that the source of everything is in me, I am never thirsty again, and I can be a source for everyone else. I realize that as I serve others, I am serving myself because we are all connected.

I believe it is essential that we wake up to a higher dimension of ourselves. We each really need to shift our identity from a separate individual personality to a soul connected to Infinite Loving Intelligence.

First, We Remember Who We Are

As we embark on this healing journey, first we remember the truth of *who* we are and *where* we are. We are infinite spiritual beings of the universe having finite human experiences. We are souls, and we have personalities. We are vibrations living in a vibrational universe. Everything is energy.

Our personalities can be the only thing we know about ourselves. This was certainly the case for me before this diagnosis of MS came as a wake-up call. I thought I was separate from my body, separate from life, and separate from everyone. I thought I had nothing to do with my body, with my thoughts, and with my life. I am realizing, in fact, I am at the center of my own experience. I am connected to my body and to life, and I can choose my thoughts.

We do not breathe ourselves; however, we can choose to breathe consciously. This brings us back into the present moment. Our only point of power lies in this present moment. There is a loving intelligence giving us our every breath, guiding us, and supporting us.

We do not make our heart beat. We do not digest our food. We do not make our hair grow. There is a power in us and all around us, and it is doing it all for us. There is a loving intelligence giving us life every moment.

Thinking happens all the time, whether we want it or not and whether we are aware of it or not. Our power lies in choosing our thoughts. Nothing matters more than what we are thinking right now. How we feel informs us of what we are thinking.

We are miracles. If you don't believe in miracles, perhaps you have forgotten you are one. The first nine months of our lives, everything was done for us. This love and support do not stop when we are born. It is ever-present. Life is ever-present to love us, support us, and guide us.

Inhale fully and exhale completely. Let us remember who we are and be grateful. Inhale deeply and exhale—let go. Let us remember where we are and be humble. Love is in us and all around us. Love is in our every breath.

Heart-Brain Coherence

The heart is connected with the soul, and the soul connects each of us to Infinite Intelligence. We can purposefully connect with the soul through intuition. Heart-brain coherence allows us to connect with intuition—it is deep intuition on demand. It harmonizes the connection between the brain and the heart.

I love listening to the Hay House World Summit. This is a free, yearly event offering one hundred audio lessons and fifteen videos from world leaders on health and wellness. During this event in 2016, I learned a way of practicing heart-brain coherence from Gregg Braden, a pioneer in bridging science and spirituality. Gregg Braden partners with the HeartMath Institute, a global nonprofit organization that helps people connect with their hearts.

There are three steps required to practice heart-brain coherence:

1. Move your attention from your head to your heart.

To make sure you really move your awareness to your heart and not just think about it, you physically touch your heart center. You can do that by:

- Putting the palm of your hand on your heart.
- Putting your hands together in prayer pose with your thumbs touching your chest.
- Putting a finger on your chest.

This turns your attention inside.

2. For at least three minutes, practice slow, deep, rhythmic breathing through your heart area.

   - Inhale for the count of five.
   - Exhale for the count of five.

   This tells your body you are safe.

3. Generate a feeling of care, appreciation, gratitude, or compassion for anything or anyone.

Once you establish this harmonized connection between your heart and your brain, that is the time to ask a question to the wisdom of your heart and access your deepest truth. First, you listen to the answer. The answer could be a sensation in your body or words you hear or something else. (For example, I get a voice inside or shivers in my body.) Then, you honor this wisdom by following it.

You can practice heart-brain coherence in the morning or at night, before an important conversation, when you want to show some love to your body, or anytime. Practicing for only three minutes produces benefits that can last for up to six hours.

Heart-brain coherence not only allows you to tune into your intuition and your subconscious mind but also allows you to tap into your creativity and your resilience—your capacity to adapt to change. This practice activates your parasympathetic nervous system and awakens the healing life-giving chemistry for more than thirteen thousand biochemicals in the immune system, cardiovascular system, and antiaging hormones.

The heart is the first organ to develop. There is a little brain in the heart. The heart possesses its own intrinsic nervous system, containing more than forty thousand sensory neurons. The magnetic field emitted from the heart is five thousand times stronger than the one from the brain.

The brain and the heart are constantly communicating with each other. This is a two-way communication: through the vagus nerve and through the spinal cord. We can learn to make them work together by harmonizing them.

It is said that the longest journey we will ever take is from our head to our heart. I began that journey. I was all in my head. I thought my heart was my greatest weakness. I am learning to tap into my greatest power—my heart.

CHAPTER 10

Precious Mysterious Life

Life is the result of the struggle between dynamic opposites /
Form and Chaos, Substance and Oblivion, Light and Dark / And
all the infinite variation of Yin and Yang / When the pendulum
swings in favor of one / It will eventually swing in favor of its
opposite / Thus the balance of the universe is maintained.
—A song by Jeru the Damaja

The Yin-Yang Symbol

Yin-Yang Theory

Everything in the universe is energy. Energy cannot be created or destroyed. It can only be transformed. This we know from science (from Einstein) and philosophy (from Taoism). Everything was created in polarities, so we live in a world of duality. Energy manifests into two complementary opposites: yin and yang, and all manifestations are temporary.

Life can be viewed through the Taoist philosophy of the yin-yang theory, represented by the symbol on the previous page. Life as a whole is illustrated by the circle. The circle symbolizes the cyclical nature of life and its unity. The circle is divided into two halves—yin (black) and yang (white).

Everything has two aspects—a yin aspect and a yang aspect. It is a model we can apply to virtually anything. Each half always describes something in relation to its opposite. Each half of the yin-yang circle contains a dot of the opposite color, meaning that each half contains its opposite. The curved line between the two halves means that these two polarities are constantly dancing with one another. This theory illustrates the constant nature of change.

In his book *The Web That Has No Weaver: Understanding Chinese Medicine*, Ted J. Kaptchuk describes: "Thus yin and yang create each other, control each other, and transform into each other."[20]

"The character for Yin originally meant the shady side of a slope. It is associated with such qualities as cold, rest, responsiveness, passivity, darkness, interiority, downwardness, inwardness, decrease, satiation, tranquility, and quiescence. It is the end, completion, and realized fruition. The original meaning of Yang was the sunny side of a slope. The term implies brightness and is part of one common Chinese expression for the sun. Yang is associated with qualities such as heat, stimulation, movement, activity, excitement, vigor, light, exteriority, upwardness, outwardness, and increase. It is arousal, beginning, and dynamic potential."[21]

Yin-Yang in Nature-Life[22]

Nature-Life	
Yang	**Yin**
sun	moon
full moon	new moon
waxing moon	waning moon
heat	cold
sun	rain
day	night
spring	fall
summer	winter
light	shadow
sky	earth
fire	water
good	bad
paradise	hell
positive	negative
future	past
evolution	involution
superior	inferior
change	stability
health	disease
birth	death

The Left Side of My Body

I love yoga in general and became a kundalini yoga teacher in 2007. A few weeks after my training ended, only one side of my body became paralyzed, and I was diagnosed with MS. Eventually, I became curious and wondered: *Why only the left side and not the right? What is the meaning?*

When I discovered yin yoga out of the blue in 2008, it was like coming home. Yin yoga is slow, gentle, and contemplative. It suited perfectly the limited physical capacities of my body at that time.

This is when the yin-yang theory started revealing itself to me. I was discovering the yin aspect of myself and of life. I was discovering the other half of myself and of life that I never knew existed. I was a very yang person and was very familiar with the yang qualities. However, I was not aware yin existed to complement yang to form a balanced whole.

Yin-Yang in a Human Being[23]

Human Being	
Yang	**Yin**
masculine energy	feminine energy
left brain	right brain
right side of the body	left side of the body
upper half of the body	lower half of the body
mind	body
thoughts	emotions
brain	heart
reason	intuition
rational	irrational
ego	soul
outer world	inner world
conscious	unconscious
visible	invisible
active	passive
inhale	exhale
give	receive
harshness	gentleness
fast	slow
do	be
spirituality	sexuality

sexuality	sensuality
act	listen

We Are Feminine and Masculine

Typically, the yin aspect is represented by a woman, and the yang aspect is represented by a man. But a man could be mostly feminine, just as a woman could be mostly masculine. These characteristics of yin and yang are not gender specific. A human being represents a whole and has both feminine energy and masculine energy—both yin and yang. I learned that to be balanced and whole, we need both polarities. It is not a matter of either or; it is a matter of this *and* that.

Yin is the feminine energy. There really was nothing feminine about me, even though I am a woman physically. Not only did I not dress feminine or express my femininity in any way, but I was also denying all the yin attributes. I had always hated to be a woman up until then. My belief was always: who would want to be a woman in this world? I grew up believing that being a woman was the worst gender a person could be and that it was a great disadvantage to be a woman. So, I did not want to have anything to do with being a woman.

I grew up literally believing women, and all yin characteristics, had no place in this world. I believed being a woman was weak and inferior—not different but inferior. I despised everything relating to the yin quality and worshipped every yang quality. I certainly wanted to be superior and strong, so I chose to be like a man and to embody all the yang traits. I had not realized that without women, none of us would be on this earth and that real strength and power in each one of us comes from the union of yin and yang.

I grew up in Africa first and then North America. Women are not equal to men in either of these places. Even if women have more recognition in Canada, women, and the yin side of life, are not fully recognized in either of these places. The world is changing and evolving, but we do not yet live in a world where the yin and yang facets of life are equal and recognized to complement each other.

Those negative and very limiting beliefs about femininity and every yin attribute manifested drastically in my body. The left side of the body represents the yin aspect compared to the right side. My left side was telling me: "*Wake up!* I exist too!" So, I started waking up to everything yin. I became curious about the yin side of everything. What was this side of everything that I had always ignored and was not even aware existed?

The body is considered the yin side, while the mind is considered the yang side. My body was the very first and most obvious thing I gave its existence back to. I began by listening to it and getting to know it by giving it some love and attention. I began with a holistic bodywork method to liberate it from all its tensions, which were preventing me from even feeling that I had a body. I never really cared that I have a body. My body was only a tool designed to get me to where my mind wanted to go. My body was only a means to an end. I never knew how intelligent it was. My body has the intelligence of life herself, as everything it does is far beyond mere human intelligence. It is a divine and perfect miracle. Now, I aim at loving my body as much as it loves me.

I denied my emotions as I believed they were as sign of weakness and served no purpose. I learned that emotions are very powerful and keep us in touch with our needs. They are life in us. They make us vulnerable, which is also what makes us authentic. Emotions are the yin side, while thoughts are the yang side. Dr. Dispenza teaches that thoughts are the language of the mind and emotions are the language of the body. Thoughts are the electrical signals that send out information to the universe, and emotions generate a magnetic field around the body, which attracts back in a person's life everything he or she is feeling. The mind, thoughts, and brain (the yang aspects) should work in harmony and coherence with the body, emotions, and heart (the yin aspects).

Most of my life, I only gave value to my rational mind, particularly my reason, as I believed in its supremacy. Of course, reason is yang, as opposed to intuition, which is yin. I did not know I had intuition, which is more powerful than reason as it connects us to Infinite Intelligence. Like emotions can seem irrational, intuition too can seem irrational and opens us to the unknown, when compared to the well-known territory of reason. It is intuition that connects us to our souls, which connect us to Infinite Intelligence. Intuition is a kind of intelligence that goes beyond the reason of our limited personalities or egos.

I was hypnotized by the outer world, and I was unaware of my inner world of thoughts and feelings. I was oblivious to the fact that I had an inner wisdom in my unconscious mind and that it is my unconscious mind that governs my life. I was ignorant of the great help available to me in my inner wisdom through my unconscious mind. I only knew about my ego. I did not know I am a soul having a human experience.

Now I know that to be whole and complete and to use all the power available to me, I can choose to embrace both polarities. I can decide to make them work in harmony with one another. I can unite these opposites in equilibrium in me. This equilibrium is ever moving. It is not something we can attain. It is something we can only aim at. There is a perpetual dance between the pairs of opposites.

This sums up everything I am learning. This shows everything that existed in life but did not exist in my life. I am forever grateful MS came to wake me up to a whole side of life I was oblivious to—the yin half of me and of life. Health is when both polarities are united in equilibrium. Life is ever seeking balance.

We Are Sexual and Spiritual

Sexuality and spirituality is another couple that offered me infinite wisdom. I never gave sexuality its own right to exist. I never recognized its vital importance in life. On my healing journey, I learned that sexuality is feminine as compared to its opposite spirituality, which is masculine. I grew up believing that sexuality is not important and denying that I am a sexual being. I believed that sexuality was inferior to spirituality. I was proud to consider myself a spiritual being, but it was an intellectual spirituality, not an embodied spirituality. I gave value only to the spiritual side of me, or so I thought.

I learned that sexuality is actually at the very basis of life. Obviously, without this sacred practice, I would not be here, as is the case with all of humanity. Through my study of the yogic anatomy, I learned that we are energy beings. We have seven chakras, or energy centers, located along the spinal column. They all play a vital role in life, health, and general well-being. The kundalini energy starts at the base of the spine at the root chakra. It is the life force, creative energy, and sexual energy. It is the most powerful energy, as it has the power to create life.

Sexuality and spirituality are two human aspects that carry many beliefs and judgments. It certainly was the case for me. But I learned through studying tantra that sexual energy and spiritual energy are the same. The spiritual energy is only more refined than the sexual energy. In the tantric tradition, the sexual energy, called Shakti, is considered feminine. We can learn to let it move up the spine so it unites at the crown of the head, where the masculine energy, called Shiva, sits. It is important to allow sexual energy. We can encourage it to move up the spine and flow through all the different chakras. As it does so, this energy increases its frequency and raises a person's level of awareness. We can choose a conscious sexuality, where we unite pleasure and passion with love and consciousness.

Like a tree, if we want strong branches to grow up toward the sky, we must develop strong roots that go deep into the earth. We cannot expect consciousness to expand if it is not well grounded in the strong foundation of the base chakra. In the chakra system and chakra chart presented on the following pages, you will find the name of each of the seven chakras with the color, power, function, and gland associated with each.

The Chakra System

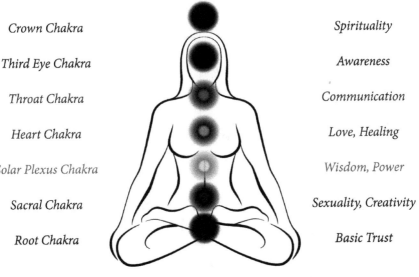

Crown Chakra	*Spirituality*
Third Eye Chakra	*Awareness*
Throat Chakra	*Communication*
Heart Chakra	*Love, Healing*
Solar Plexus Chakra	*Wisdom, Power*
Sacral Chakra	*Sexuality, Creativity*
Root Chakra	*Basic Trust*

Chakras

	Energy Center	Color	Power and Function	Glands
7	crown chakra	white or violet	spirituality and divinity	pituitary
6	third-eye chakra	indigo	intuition and vision	pineal
5	throat chakra	blue	communication and expression	thyroid
4	heart chakra	green	love, healing, and seat of the soul	thymus
3	solar plexus chakra	yellow	wisdom, will, and power	adrenal
2	sacral chakra or hara	orange	sexuality, creativity, relationships, and action	digestive and pancreatic
1	base or root chakra	red	basic trust, safety, and security	sexual

Healing Is Listening and Acting

I learned that healing can also be viewed through the yin-yang model. First, we listen to what is seeking to be heard. We listen to our intuition. We listen to the body, the still small voice, night dreams, and the synchronicities in our lives. It is important that we listen to life as life is always talking to us. It is also important to humble ourselves toward this loving power guiding our lives.

Life will begin by whispering to us. Then she will speak louder if we do not pay attention to our lives and do not listen. She will start screaming if we really do not listen. This is when the whole metaphorical brick walls of our lives can come crashing down as life begins to yell. This is all loving and for our greatest good. The message is important for us to hear. Once we do, we will have become better, wiser, and happier versions of ourselves. Learning to listen makes the message come in a gentler way.

Second, it is important that we act on what we hear, as we need to do something in order to change. And this is very personal to each one of us. What I needed to change in order to heal is not what someone else needs to change in order to heal. Our symptoms are very intelligent and precise. They are unique to each one of us. They can help guide us to understand what it is we need to know. Obviously, for me, part of healing was an invitation to embody the yin aspect of everything in me and life. Thank you, life!

SECTION 3

Forgiveness

CHAPTER 11

MS Is a Gift

You Won't Heal from Your Disease; It is
your Disease that Will Heal you.
—Carl Gustav Jung

My Understanding of MS

Life is certainly a mystery. The many reasons and ways a disease like MS manifests is also a mystery. However, I believe healing is possible, and I know healing is an inside job. It is essential to look within. The cure is inside, not outside. The following is my understanding of how and why multiple sclerosis manifests based on my personal journey and studies that I share with you in this book.

Marie Lise Labonté teaches that it takes three stressful events for a disease to manifest in the body. This is based in psychosomatic knowledge. Please refer to her book: *Le déclic: Transformer la douleur qui détruit en douleur qui guérit*, page 66. The first stressful event can happen as early as conception. I am referring to a perceived shock or trauma that we are not able to digest and process. The same stressful event can happen to two different people and not lead to the same outcome. It all depends on each person's perception and how he or she deals with the event.

Stress can happen in our lives that we may not know how to handle. Then we may start thinking and feeling the same contractive thoughts and emotions. These repeated stresses will eventually manifest in the body, creating tensions and leading to disease. These bodily tensions, limited emotions, and contractive beliefs all lower our vibration and continually signal the same gene in the same way. As a result, we stop moving forward in life and remain stuck at the time the stressful event happened because the body and the mind are stuck in the past. I believe the gene for MS becomes activated as a result of this process. The physical manifestation of the disease and diagnosis follow. It is mostly an unconscious process.

Dr. Dispenza gives an example of this process: "If at some point in your past you were shocked, betrayed, or traumatized by an event with a high emotional charge that has left you feeling pain or sadness or fear, chances are that experience has been branded into your biology in numerous ways. It's also possible that the genes that were activated by this experience might keep your body from healing. So in order for you to change your body into a new genetic expression, the inner emotion you create has to be greater than the emotion from that past outer experience. The energy of your empowerment or the amplitude of your inspiration must be greater than your pain or sadness. Now you are changing the inner environment of the body, which is the outer environment of the cell; the genes for heath can be up-regulated while the genes for disease can be down-regulated. The more profound the emotion, the louder you're knocking on your genetic door and the more you're going to signal those genes to change the structure and function of your body. That's how it works."[24]

We know today from the new science of epigenetics that it is not genes that create disease. It is the environment—more specifically, emotions—that dictates which gene will be expressed to create health or disease. Emotions are the results or end products of experiences in our inner or outer environments. Epigenetics is a new and exciting area of research. It literally means "above genetics."

We are not victims of our genes. Our genes respond to our inner and outer environments. We can change the expression of our genes by changing our emotions. We can influence the outer environment by having experiences that produce elevated emotions. We can control the inner environment by becoming aware of the inner state of being and creating an elevated one with our thoughts and feelings. First, we liberate suppressed limited emotions from the body. This raises its frequency and brings it back into the present moment. Second, we choose life-giving thoughts and elevated emotions that carry a high vibration.

Dr. Dispenza teaches us, according to the quantum model of reality, that "All disease is a lowering of frequency and an incoherent message."[25] This model recognizes that reality is 99.99999 percent energy and 0.00001 percent matter. He says: "Our personality is how we think, how we feel, and how we act, and it creates our personal reality." We can become new people by thinking new thoughts, feeling new emotions, and behaving in new ways. We then stop signaling the same gene that activated the disease and start signaling new genes for health.

We can choose the programs in the unconscious mind that run our lives. We can decide to change them if they do not produce results we love. If they produce or trigger a disease like MS, we can decide to change from the inside out. When we correct the inside, the outside will reflect that change, as the outside is always a perfect reflection of the inside. We live in an inside out universe.

MS Is Healing

After I graduated from my kundalini yoga teacher training course in 2007, my body tried to heal itself through a first crisis of MS. During my training, I learned a whole new way of being, opposite from the one I was raised in. I ended up at the hospital for my twenty-ninth birthday. I tried to pay no attention to this loud calling. I ignored these coincidences of me getting sick right after I graduated and on my birthday. I chose to believe the universe made a horrible mistake, and I was only its poor victim. This disease made no sense to me. I really thought that was the worst thing that could happen to me. In fact, I came to realize that not listening to my intuition was the worst thing that could ever have happened to me. I tried to go on with my life as if nothing had happened without making any changes. I tried denial for three years.

After I graduated from my kripalu yoga teacher training course in 2010, my body tried to heal itself again through a second crisis of MS. I ended up at the hospital for my thirty-second birthday. I wondered what these coincidences were. Why was I, once again, at the hospital right after I graduated and for my birthday? This was so severe. My life was so torn apart that it finally got my attention. I was now willing to open myself to what was. I was ready to listen to the message trying to make its way to my conscious mind. I surrendered to life. That was the best thing that happened to me.

I learned from Dr. Soulier's DVD, *Sortir de la sclérose en plaques*, which means "coming out of multiple sclerosis," and from a workshop with him that it is fairly common that MS is triggered the moment people make a *good* decision for themselves and move out of the system they were raised in. The old belief system is then confronted with a different reality. That moment could be the end or the beginning of some studies, the beginning of a career, moving to a new place, traveling abroad, an engagement, or a wedding. Obviously, this is what happened to me—twice after a graduation and on my birthday—the moment I discovered life can be lived according to a belief system that was not the same as the one I was raised in. But instead of interpreting this manifestation in my body as my body trying to heal itself by adapting to the new belief system yoga was offering me, I kept the old system in place. Thus, I remained stuck for many years because I did not understand what was happening and didn't try to find the meaning of the event.

Dr. Soulier gives a great example in his DVD. He compares the body to an electric appliance used to running on 120-volt current. The moment you plug the appliance into 220-volt current—which is the moment your life seems to be headed in the right direction following a good decision you've made—the body is overwhelmed and crashes, just like an electric appliance would if plugged into a higher current. The old system comes to a stop.

He explains that MS could start as soon as the first cells develop in the embryo. MS can also happen when the person fails to go through the normal teenage rebellion period to find his or her own voice and end parental submission. He points to the fact that MS is an autoimmune disease, reflecting an inner identity conflict between the real self and the false self—the learned self.

The way out of MS is to stop being a continuation of our parents and to start to embody our real identities by becoming the unique individuals we are meant to be. We become independent and think for ourselves by finding our own belief systems. We leave the family and the group to find our own voices, which is the goal of the individuation process. In fact, what is happening—the crisis—is good news. It is an opportunity to move away from what was not us to become more of who we were meant to be. This is why I think this disease is an attempt to heal—because it usually happens the moment we make some sort of good decision for our lives.

Give people a chance to experience their suffering so they can evolve. We need our struggles to evolve. Have compassion for them and help them. I received a lot of help on my journey to try to find the meaning of what was happening. Also allow people to find the gift in what is happening. Know that life is perfect and that "life loves you," as Louise Hay says. If this happens, it is happening for you. Look for the good. There is good in everything that happens. "Every adversity, every failure, every heartache carries with it the seed of an equal or greater benefit," says Napoleon Hill, author of the book *Think and Grow Rich*. That seed has to be found, planted, and nurtured.

MS Healed Me

My healing journey made me aware of my miraculous body. I did not know I had an intelligent body. My body was lost under all its physical tensions, suppressed emotions, and limiting beliefs. I learned that my body is not a machine. Rather, my body is a miracle and is divinely intelligent. I can always rely on it because it never lies. My body is a precious ally.

My healing journey made me aware of my intelligent emotions. In the past, I was not aware that my emotions served a purpose, and I believed they were a sign of weakness. I did not know that if I allowed my emotions to flow through me, they would be short-lived. Now I know my emotions are guides to assist my journey through life and to inform me of my needs. When I began liberating them, gave myself permission to feel them, and allowed them to flow through me, I became more alive and felt guided. It is a strength to express my emotions, and they are precious allies.

My healing journey made me aware of my powerful conscious mind. I had been completely unconscious. I was not aware that I was continuously thinking and that I have the power to choose my thoughts. I did not know I could choose to be an active participant in my life. I can create heaven or hell in my mind. I can be my own worst enemy, or I can be my own best friend. I get to choose. My conscious mind in a precious ally.

My healing journey made we aware of my loving and powerful unconscious mind. I did not know I have a loving intelligence working day and night for me. I did not know so much love was available for me, in me, and all around me. I now feel so supported and guided. My healing journey made me aware that my unconscious mind is always here to help me, to heal me, and to make me whole and unique. My unconscious mind is a precious loving ally.

My healing journey made me aware of my loving soul. I am more than my personality—I am a soul having a finite human experience. My soul has been with me all of my life, patiently waiting for me to reconnect with it and listen to it. It is always guiding me and softly whispering to me through my intuition. My soul is a precious loving ally.

MS made me aware that I live in a conscious, loving universe. I now know that the universe is alive and that there is a loving intelligence in me and all around me. I now know that this universe is loving and perfect. The universe is my most loving and powerful ally.

My healing journey invited me to become whole and complete. I learned that wholeness is the result of the union of yin and yang in me. In my journey toward healing, I am learning to become the unique person I am and to fall in love with myself and with life. The day I accepted what was happening *for* me was the day everything started to change. The moment I allowed life to break me open was the day life opened up for me.

"The cure for pain is in the pain," Rumi said.
"A disease is a call to healing," Carl Gustav Jung said.

"The crack is where the light enters," Leonard Cohen said.
"When you encounter an obstacle on your journey toward God, know that God is hiding within the obstacle waiting for you," the Kabbalah says.

A Voice During Kirtan

I have been attending kirtan on and off since I discovered yoga in 2003. Kirtan is the yoga of voice. It is chanting in the form of call-and-response, where the singer sings a mantra and others repeat it. It is usually in Sanskrit; however, it could also be in another language. I found it is an excellent experience that helps me quiet my mind. It invites me to focus my mind on a word or a phrase that carries a high vibration and a particular message. I still find it to be a beautiful and peaceful practice that I love. For example, one classic mantra we often sing at the beginning of a class is "Om Gum Ganapatayei Namaha." It is a salutation to the Hindu god Ganesh, which is the remover of obstacles.

About five years after my second MS crisis in 2010, one night I attended a kirtan meditation. During the class, between two songs, I received the thought: *MS is a gift.* I was very shocked at first by this very irrational idea. But by this time, I was not only still very rational but my healing journey led me to realize I am also very intuitive. Now I listen to my still small voice that can sound so irrational.

Just before I had my first MS crisis in 2007, I was very unhappy and desperate to find a deeper and more profound way to live my life. I had asked life to guide me to more, and a few weeks later, after my kundalini yoga teacher training had ended, I was diagnosed with MS. I never expected to find a gift under such dramatic circumstances. It is the gift that took me the longest to unwrap and the most poorly wrapped gift ever. I would eventually discover it would be the most precious gift.

When I heard that irrational idea, it made me wonder and question my beliefs around MS. It made me take an honest look at the results my inner work of the previous years had produced. My body had been stuck in the past under physical tensions, suppressed emotions, and limiting beliefs. I brought it back to the present moment. I was able to be reborn after all those years into a better version of myself. I received the most precious gift: *me*. I believe life is a gift and that everything is a gift. MS was a gift for me because it led me to heal myself. I started to listen to my body, my emotions, my conscious and unconscious mind, my soul, and life. MS became a gift after much education and work on myself.

CHAPTER 12

Gratitude

If the Only Prayer You Say in your life is
'Thank you,' That Would Suffice.
—Meister Eckhart

Gratitude for Everything

Gratitude and nonjudgment go together. Gratitude opens the door to nonjudgment. It has a lot to do with my perception. How can I really know in my limited human mind if something is good or bad? Something simply is. Is it good? Is it bad? I came to realize that I really don't know.

Everything is neutral from the point of view of my soul. I assign meaning to events, situations, and circumstances. I control my perception. I can judge something as good when, in reality, it is not as good as it appears to be. The reverse is also true. I can judge something as bad when, in reality, it could be a blessing in disguise.

This is exactly what happened to me. At first, I thought MS was the worst thing that could happen to me. I came to realize that the worst thing that happened to me was not listening my intuition. This has been a huge lesson of my life. I am learning to listen to life's precise Infinite Loving Intelligence.

Then, I thought MS was the best thing that happened to me because ultimately it led to my healing. In fact, the best thing that happened to me from this experience was learning to surrender to life. When I realized that I am not in control of life, I began to develop a humble attitude. I became aware that life is in control, and I began to surrender to her.

MS was not the worst thing that happened to me, and it wasn't the best thing that happened for me. MS is just something that happened. My healing journey gave me the gift of a neutral mind. I am human, and I am quick to judge. However, I am also a soul with the power to pause my judgment and to let the good in any situation reveal itself to me.

I know that when I don't understand the meaning of an event, I can still be grateful in the midst of it. I can trust that its meaning will be revealed to me in the future. I can trust that it is happening for the evolution of my soul—the evolution of my consciousness.

An attitude of gratitude helps me accept the present moment. If it contains something pleasant, gratitude invites me to fully savor it and take in the good. If it contains something less pleasing, gratitude invites me to pause my judgment so I can find the good in whatever is happening. Coming from a place of gratitude helps me trust that the good in any situation will reveal itself to me.

Abundance

Gratitude is a powerful emotion that carries a very high vibration. It allows for the recognition of the abundance already present inside me and all around me. Gratitude is on the same frequency as abundance. Gratitude is a practice.

We know from Einstein that "We cannot solve our problems with the same level of thinking that created them." We can decide to change our thinking to solve a problem, situation, or circumstance we are facing. Our thinking dictates our emotions, which are our conscious awareness of the vibrations we are in. We can decide to raise our vibrations to find a way out of a problem. Gratitude is an accessible and efficient way to raise our vibrations.

Gratitude is available for me as there is always more right than wrong with me. I am alive. I am breathing. Every breath that keeps me alive is given to me. I start with the recognition of this precious gift of life that I have the privilege to experience. I am blessed, and I am grateful for this life.

The more I focus on the good I already have, the more I attract good in my life. The more I live in a state of gratitude, the happier I feel. The list of things to be grateful for is endless. I strive to be grateful for everything because everything has a gift in it.

There is a practice of keeping a daily gratitude journal. I did for many years. When I do, I become more aware and notice more the things that I can be grateful for that come my way during the day.

Cultivating gratitude helps me move my attention to what I have instead of my very normal human tendency to focus on what I don't have. Gratitude opens my heart and connects me with my capacity to be in awe. Life is a miracle. I am a miracle. I can be grateful for everything because everything is a miracle. I choose my perception. Albert Einstein said: "There are only two ways to live your life. One is as though nothing is a miracle. The other is as though everything is a miracle."

Out of gratitude, joy arises, regardless of conditions and inclusive of all circumstances—the simple joy of being, the profound gratitude to be alive and to recognize it is a gift and a miracle.

CHAPTER 13

Faith

Father, if you are willing, take this cup from me;
yet not my will, but yours be done.
—Luke 22:42 (New International Version)

Fear or Love

The meaning of this quote: "not my will, but yours be done," for me
is that there is a higher power who knows and guides everything
and everyone. This power knows what is best.

The key to my healing was opening to something greater than
my rational mind, to something I cannot explain or comprehend,
and to surrender to it. I like to simply call it life—Infinite Loving
Intelligence. I can also call it love or spirit or grace or God. It is the
unknown. I am learning, more and more, to open to its presence, to
listen to it, to lean in, and to surrender to it. I am learning to partner
with this power. This power is in me.

"The most important decision we make is whether we believe we
live in a friendly or hostile universe," Albert Einstein said. I choose
to believe in the power of love.

Marie Lise Labonté

Marie Lise Labonté was the first person to open me up to something greater than my rational mind and to something beyond what my eyes could see. She is a spiritual mother to me. I love her and am forever grateful to her. With her, I reconnected with my soul and was born to the spiritual side of myself. I started waking up to the fact that I am a spiritual being having a human experience.

The first time I met Marie Lise Labonté in 2010, I learned to my surprise that she is also a medium. She channels messages from the Mother Soul, Xedah, and Maitreya. I was shocked when she told us she would go into a trance. Mediums had not been a part of my reality prior to this. A medium communicates with another dimension. Anything outside this three-dimensional reality that most of us live in did not exist for me. That was the beginning of me opening beyond my reason. This opening and surrendering to the unknown has no end.

When I attended a seminar with Marie Lise Labonté the following year, I remembered my soul. During a break, I went for a walk and memories from my childhood came back to my conscious mind. I remembered my innocence and my connection to this higher dimension of myself.

Pierre Lessard

Pierre Lessard is a man who channels an entity called Master St-Germain. I met him in Montreal where he gives public channelings. I attended one of his spiritual vacation retreats in the Dominican Republic in 2014.

He taught me that I can choose the joy of being me and that my joy begins by being myself. It is essential in the healing process to become ourselves. We can all choose the joy of being ourselves. I consciously chose the joy of being me in the Dominican Republic during this spiritual vacation. We all took this vow out load as a closing ritual of the retreat.

Learning that it was desirable to be myself was important for me. In the past, I had always felt so different from the norm, and I always had a hard time following the masses. However, I still was not able to accept myself or be myself. It was such relief for me to learn that I could be me and allow everyone else to be themselves. The only thing we are sure to succeed in is being ourselves. We are all unique, we all have special gifts, and we all have special purposes only we can fulfill. It is essential that we all be our unique authentic selves.

Esther Hicks

Esther Hicks is a woman who channels a consciousness called Abraham. I found her teachings to be very helpful, as have millions of people. She teaches about the law of attraction around the world. She has written many books and produced numerous videos, and many of her teachings can be found on YouTube.

The law of attraction simply states: like energy attracts like energy. We are energy, and we attract what we give out. Just like the law of gravity, the law of attraction is always in action. It did not begin the day I became aware of its existence. It has always been controlling my life; I just did not know it.

The law of attraction is a law of the universe. It is activated through attention, intention, and expectation. It is invoked with desire for something and expectation of receiving that thing. So, you create an intention for what you want, and you keep your attention on it. Where you put your attention is where your energy flows. Then you expect to receive that thing and act as if it is already yours. Expectation of receiving is key to getting anything in life.

John of God: Thirty-Sixth Birthday

While I was doing my holistic bodywork training, I took a hot bath almost every day. I wanted to feel good and relax my body. While I was doing this, I would always listen to some uplifting video to feed my mind and my soul with inspiring knowledge. More often than not, I would listen to Dr. Wayne Dyer, whom I absolutely love. I found such inspiration in his words. He taught me that "if I Change the way I look at things, the things I look at change." This turned out to be so true in my life.

There is an infinite number of his videos on YouTube. In one of these videos, he shares about his experience of a remote healing by the Brazilian healer John of God. He was living in Hawaii, and John of God was living in Brazil. Dr. Dyer received a spiritual intervention while he was in his home in Maui, and he was also instructed to take some herbs. Afterward, he was healed. This blew my mind because this was so out of my known reality.

John of God is a spiritual healer. He has touched the lives of millions of people around the world. He says it is not him, but it is God who heals. I became really curious about this healer. I thought this healing was possible for someone so famous as Dr. Wayne Dyer, but not for an unknown woman like me. How could I possibly find him in a huge country like Brazil? So, I dismissed it as a possibility for myself.

One day in 2014, I was doing my holistic bodywork training. A woman in my group named Renée Langlois had just gotten back from seeing John of God in Brazil. I was amazed. What were the odds? With her help, I was able to make my fantasy a reality. She told me that John of God was in Abadiania, Brazil. I found a guide who helped me make the trip to see him.

Renée gave me two books to read before seeing this spiritual healer:
- *Gail Thackray's Spiritual Journeys: Visiting John of God* by Gail Thackray
- *John of God: The Brazilian Healer Who's Touched the Lives of Millions* by Heather Cumming and Karen Leffler

My guide also gave me three books to read before meeting John of God:
- *You Can Heal Your Life* by Louise Hay
- *The Four Agreements: A Practical Guide to Personal Freedom* by Don Miguel Ruiz
- *Your Soul's Plan: Discovering the Real Meaning of the Life You Planned Before You Were Born* by Robert Schwartz

I arrived in the city of Abadiania on the day of my thirty-sixth birthday. I had a list of all the requests I wanted to present him, which included, of course, healing from MS. He heals with a spiritual surgery or a physical surgery, and each person is given the choice. I chose the spiritual surgery. A surgery is an intervention. It means a change in direction in life.

MS came to show me that I was not on my path but on someone else's path. To heal means to find my own path as I listen to life in me, which means listening to my intuition, staying in touch with what I would love, and following my bliss.

The spiritual surgery happened in a room where a group of people gathered. John of God channels more than thirty entities, which are people who have passed. Some of the entities are doctors, and it is the entities who performed the healing. We prayed as the healing happened, focusing on our intention. After the spiritual surgery, I remained in my room for twenty-four hours to rest. I also took herbs and followed a few guidelines for forty days: no spicy food or peppers, no fertilized eggs, no vigorous exercise, and no sexual arousal.

When I initially entered the room to meet him, the song that was playing was one of my favorite songs from my kundalini yoga teacher training course. The song is "Anand" from Snatam Kaur. *Anand* means bliss. What a so-called coincidence that one of my favorite songs was playing at that exact moment.

When I had the spiritual surgery, I started to remember everything. I remembered that I am always guided. I am never alone in this infinite loving universe. During the surgery, I had the most intense emotional release. I cried so much and let go of years of suffering. After the surgery, I felt peaceful and surrendered completely to God. I also stopped having to use a stick to walk.

In their DVD, *Co-Creating at Its Best: A Conversation Between Master Teachers*, Esther Hicks (or Abraham more precisely) explains to Dr. Dyer that it is our very high expectation of being healed that make the healing happen. We actually do not need an intermediate to heal. We are all connected to God.

CHAPTER 14

Love

Love is the Essence of Life, the Universe and Everything.
—Unknown

Self-Love

This diagnosis of MS really invited me to love myself unconditionally. I never understood how crucial it is to love myself. I was aware of the very popular saying "love your neighbor as yourself," but I only understood it halfway. Love your neighbor, sure. But I completely disregarded the part "as yourself." But it is a critical part. Self-love is something we can learn. It is something I learned and continue to deepen.

I grew up believing that to love myself is selfish. But how can I truly love another if I do not love myself first? Everything starts with me, and everything comes from me. I am at the center of my own life. My priority is to love and honor the precious being that I am. Then I can love and honor other precious beings. I had it all upside down.

In planes, you are instructed to put the oxygen mask on yourself first, even before your children. How can I love others and be of service to them if I do not love and serve myself first? It sounds so simple and obvious, but that was not my belief. Now I know better—I take care of myself first, so I can take better care of others.

When I was in the hospital for the second time in 2010, I was learning to walk again with my physiotherapist. We would walk around in a big room filled with mirrors. One time she suggested I smile at my image when I walked in front of a mirror. I was shocked by this idea and hated it. I did not want to see myself. Very reluctantly, I tried a shy, not so sincere smile at myself. That was really hard. How could I love and trust myself after having brought myself to the hospital? I did not love myself, and I felt I had betrayed myself and let myself down. At first, it was difficult to look at myself, let alone smile at myself. What did I have to smile about?

With the fake smile that I gave myself, I opened the door to a whole new relationship with myself. The only relationship I am in, every moment of my life, and the most precious relationship I can ever have is a relationship with myself. It's also the only relationship I know for sure I will have for the rest of my life. Now when I walk by a mirror, I smile at myself, and I give myself a compliment. I am my best friend, and I am the love of my life.

Then one day, I found mirror work with Louise Hay. I learned to look at myself in the eyes in front of the mirror and say to myself: "I love you. I really love you!" I learned to find the inner child in me and tell myself: "I love you. I really love you!" Healing comes from loving ourselves.

The more I realize I am a miracle of life and perfection, the more I fall in love with myself. I remember I was born a miracle, and I recognize *who* I am—I am an infinite, powerful, unique, and magnificent being of the universe. I also recognize *whose* I am—I am a child of the universe.

"It is my privilege and honor to love myself," says Shakti Gawain.

"Nobody can love me more than I love myself," says James Van Praagh.

"There is only one thing that heals every problem, and that is: to know how to love yourself," says Louise Hay.

Heal Yourself

I learned during my holistic bodywork training that there are common wounds every human being has when he or she is born. We all receive at least one. This wound is in the body and in the unconscious mind. We will attract everything in life to match this energy that we carry. This is the law of attraction in action. What we need to heal will rise up for us to heal. Those wounds are: abandonment, rejection, nonrecognition, betrayal, abuse, humiliation, injustice, and the obligation to be happy.

You can develop your own inner parents as you grow up. You can learn to be loving parents for your inner child. When you feel a wound, you can apply the following attitudes and give your inner child whatever it needs.

- Loving yourself means not abandoning yourself. Loving yourself is being present with yourself. It is developing a sense of your own presence and finding a sense of security within yourself.
- Loving yourself means not rejecting yourself and not judging yourself. Loving yourself is welcoming and embracing yourself completely as you are. It is accepting all the different parts of yourself—your strengths and your weaknesses.
- Loving yourself means recognizing yourself and your very own existence. It is acknowledging all that you are, all that you do, and all of your accomplishments. It is recognizing who you really are.

- Loving yourself means not betraying yourself. Loving yourself is being committed, having confidence, and trusting yourself.
- Loving yourself means not abusing yourself physically or mentally or both. Loving yourself is being kind and gentle with yourself.
- Loving yourself means not humiliating yourself. Loving yourself is respecting and honoring your very nature and self-identity.
- Loving yourself means treating yourself with justice and fairness.
- Loving yourself means not forcing yourself to be happy. Loving yourself is allowing yourself to feel whatever it is you are feeling and to be authentic.

Love

I used to be scared of other people and preferred to be alone. I felt uncomfortable and threatened in the presence of others because I felt they were all so different from me. I used to see only personalities. I used to be scared of myself and uncomfortable in my own presence because I did not know myself. I was trapped in my personality.

It is true that in our personalities we are all so very different and unique. I think this diversity is what makes us so rich as human beings. However, in our essence, we are all the same. This is one of the many paradoxes of life. "Recognize that the other person is you," says Yogi Bhajan in the first sutra of the Aquarian age. This is quite a magical and profound truth.

The five sutras of the Aquarian age as presented by Yogi Bhajan:[26]
    1. Recognize that the other person is you.
    2. There is a way through every block.

3. When the time is on you, start, and the pressure will be off.
4. Understand through compassion or you will misunderstand the times.
5. Vibrate the cosmos, the Cosmos shall clear the path.

The Aquarian age is a period that began in 2012; it is the age of awareness and enlightenment. It is the time when we take responsibility and begin to look inside for our power. I had always been looking outside of myself for my power. In the period before the Aquarian age, the Piscean age, we believed that our power and God were outside of us. MS truly led me to discover that my power is inside me.

What I have experienced is that as my love for myself grows, my love for others grows. Unconditional love for ourselves leads naturally to unconditional love for others. When I started to love myself, it was magical—I naturally started to love other people. I really could feel that it was the same thing. Pema Chödrön says: "Unconditional compassion for ourselves leads naturally to unconditional compassion for others."

I recognize that other people are all different aspects of myself, showing me that we are all one. I can love someone and choose not to be in his or her presence. I can still bless that person and thank him or her for being my teacher and then let that person go on his or her way. We all have our affinities and preferences. Yogi Bhajan says: "If you can't see God in all, you can't see God at all."

When I encounter someone who elicits an adverse reaction in me, that person is only being a mirror for what is also in me. He or she is showing me a shadow or unconscious part of myself. Instead of reacting to the other person and making that reaction all about him or her, I use this information to become more conscious of myself, to get to know myself better, and to befriend a part of myself I did not know I had. I practice nonjudgment and compassion for myself and for the other person.

When I encounter someone who elicits admiration in me, the same truth applies. The other person is only mirroring a quality I have that I might not be conscious of yet. I can cultivate this quality in myself because this attribute is also in me; that is why I can notice it in someone else. We usually do not see ourselves, but we can see another person.

We each have a unique personality. We each have our own gender, race, religion or lack of religion, culture, personal story, title, age, sexual orientation, and beliefs. We are each unique in all those outer aspects. However, we are all spiritual beings having a brief and precious human experience. We all want to be happy and avoid suffering. We come from the same source, and we return to the same source. Inside, at our core, we are all the same.

I was fortunate to be born into a family with quite a bit of diversity. My parents came from different continents, spoke different languages, and had different religions. My father is a brown man from Mauritania, and my mother is a white woman from Canada. My father is an Arabic-speaking Muslim, and my mother is a French-speaking Catholic.

How could I ever choose one over the other? One is not good and the other bad. When I was very young, I was presented with this challenge of trying to find what unites us instead of what separates us. Very early I was guided to union instead of separation and toward the attitude of this *and* that rather than this *or* that. Love had united my parents who seemed to be such opposites. I want to unite the opposites in me.

Forgiveness

Forgiveness is such a powerful practice. It is a practice because it is something we do now and forever after. Forgiveness is an act of pure, unconditional love for ourselves, and we work at forgiveness in order to set ourselves free.

Forgiveness is for us and has nothing to do with the other person. The other person does not even have to know. Forgiveness has nothing to do with condoning the behavior. It is giving up the hope of changing the past. It does not require that the other person become our friend or that we invite him or her in our home or at our table. It simply means we free ourselves from that person and what he or she did.

When you feel resentment for someone, the only person suffering is yourself. Buddha says: "Holding on to anger is like grasping a hot coal with the intent of throwing it at someone else; you are the one who gets burned." We are all human beings with imperfections, and we are all doing the best we can with our current level of understanding, knowledge, and awareness.

The first people we forgive are our parents or caregivers. It is soothing to realize they did the best they could with what they knew, which was what their parents taught them. And what our grandparents knew was the best they knew, which they learned from their parents. And on and on we can go back this way forever. There is no point in blaming anyone; it does not serve us. It keeps us stuck where we are and is a powerless position. We can choose to practice compassion instead of blame.

We can forgive another being and set ourselves free. The energy we spent in resentment we can now use in a more constructive way. We can be more loving and more creative. We can remember that the other person, just like us, is an infinite being having all that he or she needs inside. We can bless that person and let him or her go.

Louise Hay said: "Forgiveness is a gift to yourself. It frees you from the past: past experiences, and past relationships. It allows you to live in the present time. When you forgive yourself and forgive others, you are indeed free." It is safe to forgive yourself and forgive others. What we wish for others, we wish for ourselves.

Ho'oponopono

This is a Hawaiian forgiveness practice. As I realize the power of my thoughts and my words, I realize the power of this practice. We can mentally repeat the following mantra:

I am sorry.
Please forgive me.
Thank you.
I love you.

We can simply repeat these words out loud or in our minds. When I practice, I like to imagine I am repeating these affirmations to different people. I could say these words to my inner child; to my past, present, or future self; to one of my parents; to any person; to life; or to God. I find it helps me release suppressed emotions and brings me peace inside.

Loving Kindness Meditation

We can practice the following version of a loving kindness meditation. I learned it from Mary Morrissey, who learned it from his holiness, the Dalai Lama.

To practice, bring to mind someone you love, which could be a person or a pet. Then repeat this prayer:

May you be happy.
May you be at peace.
May you walk in ways that bring blessings.
May you know love.

Now bring to mind someone you want to forgive and repeat the same prayer:

May you be happy.
May you be at peace.
May you walk in ways that bring blessings.
May you know love.

For yourself, now repeat the same words:

May I be happy.
May I be at peace.
May I walk in ways that bring blessings.
May I know love.

Now extend the prayer to every being:

May we be happy.
May we be at peace.
May we walk in ways that bring blessings.
May we know love.

CHAPTER 15

Food Does Matter

Let Food Be Thy Medicine and Medicine by Thy Food.
—Hippocrates

Eat Natural Food

The yogic attitude teaches us that we eat to live and not live to eat. We are what we eat and think. The food we eat is the raw material with which our bodies build new cells and repair themselves. It is recommended that we eat food that is full of life and rich with vitamins, enzymes, and minerals that our bodies need to grow, maintain, and restore themselves. It is also important that we avoid processed food as much as possible. Louise Hay says it best in such a simple way: "If it grows, eat it. If it doesn't grow, don't eat it."

It is best that we eat a wide variety of food that includes every color of the rainbow. It will help provide us with all the different vitamins, enzymes, and minerals we need. It is also beautiful and fun. Food writer and activist Michael Pollan advises: "Eat food, not too much, mostly plants." As Maya Angelou says: "Moderation in all things. And even moderation in moderation."

The food we eat has a real influence on how we feel. Pay attention to the reaction of your body and mind when you eat. How do you feel after eating an extra-large, greasy, salty, and sugary meal? How do you feel after eating a light, colorful, and natural meal? Notice: is it the same, or is there a difference?

The body is a temple with which the sacred being moves around in this physical reality. The more I realize this, the more I want to feed it the best natural food I can find. As my love for myself grows, so does my desire to feed my body living and nourishing, real food. The more I love myself, the more I want to express this love for my body by feeding it divinely. It is one way that I have to love and honor my body.

Immune System in Our Gut

My healing journey led me to discover that not only is there a brain in the head, but there is also a brain in the heart and a brain in the gut. I learned that 70 percent of the immune system is in the intestines. We are more bacterial than we are human, as we have ten times more bacteria in the gut than cells in the body. So, it does matter what we put in our bodies. We don't want to live on food that could trigger inflammation in the gut, which could lead to inflammation in the brain.

I avoid sugar. Sugar is a drug more addictive than cocaine. It also feeds the bad bacteria in the gut. We can choose to be mindful of what we eat and read labels. Sugar is literally added to everything and goes under so many names. Eating natural food makes it much easier to avoid sugar.

I know that what I think matters way more than what I eat. The bottom line is to listen to your body. Everyone is different.

Afterword

Everything in Life is a Gift in the End And if it Does Not Feel like
a Gift Right Now It Means You Haven't Reached the End Yet.
—Anita Moorjani

Life speaks to you every moment. You can decide to listen to her guidance, trust it, and follow it. You can develop your listening skills, your faith in life, and your courage to follow your intuition as you deepen your partnership with life. To heal, you can choose to become someone else—your authentic self. The disease was in the old personality; you can decide to embody a new personality.

Looking back, I can connect the dots and see how guided I have always been. Looking forward, I can lean on life to guide me as I listen to her through my intuition.

I now listen to my body, my emotions, my conscious and unconscious mind, my soul, and life. Now I am one with life, and I learn to live in alignment with her. This adventure has helped me discover that my power is inside. I have the power to choose my thoughts and my reaction to my circumstances. I have the power to create my reality—I create with my thoughts, feelings, and actions. I am a powerful cocreator with life.

MS has been the greatest gift of my life. It has given me the gift of *me*. It has taught me to love myself. It has taught me that I am the love of my life and the most important person in my life.

Now I know that I have a body that loves me, and healing is what it does best. All I want to do now is support it in doing its marvelous job of always healing itself. My body is a miracle.

Now I know that I have emotions that are life in me. I now allow my emotions to flow through me. I feel and express them. I listen to them as they express my needs, and I do my best to honor those needs.

Now I know that I have a left brain and a right brain—reason and intuition. I have a powerful mind—a conscious mind and an unconscious mind. I master my conscious mind, and I listen to the wisdom of my unconscious mind through my dreams at night and the synchronicities in my life.

Now I know that I am an infinite spiritual being having a finite human experience—I am a soul. I trust that everything happens *for* me and the evolution of my soul. I trust life to guide me from my birth to my death.

Now I open myself to an Infinite Loving Intelligence guiding and orchestrating this whole universe. I listen to the wisdom of my divine body. I allow the wisdom of my emotions. I receive the wisdom of my conscious and unconscious mind. I trust in the divine wisdom of my soul. I am grateful!

Endnotes

1   Louise Hay, *You Can Heal Your Life* (New York: Hay House, Inc., 1984), chap. 7, Kindle.
2   Louise Hay, Ahlea Khadro, and Heather Dane, *Loving Yourself to Great Health: Thoughts & Food—the Ultimate Diet* (New York: Hay House, Inc., 2014), chap. 1, Kindle.
3   Lissa Rankin, *Mind Over Medicine: Scientific Proof That You Can Heal Yourself* (New York: Hay House, Inc., 2013), chap. 3, Kindle.
4   Herbert Benson, *The Relaxation Response* (New York: HarperTorch, 2000), 12.
5   Lissa Rankin, *Mind Over Medicine: Scientific Proof That You Can Heal Yourself* (New York: Hay House, Inc., 2013), chap. 8, Kindle.
6   Joe Dispenza, *You Are the Placebo: Making Your Mind Matter* (New York: Hay House, Inc., 2014), chap. 6, Kindle.
7   Robert A. Johnson, *Inner Work: Using Dreams and Active Imagination for Personal Growth* (New York: HarperOne, 1989), 11.
8   Wallace D. Wattles, *The Science of Getting Rich* (New York: Penguin Books, 1910), 24.
9   Joe Dispenza, *Breaking the Habit of Being Yourself: How to Lose Your Mind and Create a New One* (New York: Hay House, Inc., 2012), Chap. 3, Kindle.
10 Ibid.
11 Swami Prabhavananda and Christopher Isherwood, *How to Know God: The Yoga Aphorisms of Patanjali* (Hollywood: Vedanta Society, 1952), 57.
12 Ibid, 65.
13 Louise Hay, *You Can Heal Your Life* (New York: Hay House, Inc., 1984), chap. 15, Kindle.
14 Joe Dispenza, *Breaking the Habit of Being Yourself: How to Lose Your Mind and Create a New One* (New York: Hay House, Inc., 2012), Introduction, Kindle.
15 David R. Hawkins, *Healing and Recovery* (New York: Hay House, Inc., 2013), chap. 1, Kindle.
16 Ibid, chap. 4, Kindle.
17 Ibid, chap. 2, Kindle.
18 Ibid, chap. 4, Kindle.

19 Joe Dispenza, *Breaking the Habit of Being Yourself: How to Lose Your Mind and Create a New One* (New York: Hay House, Inc., 2012), Afterword, Kindle.

20 Ted J. Kaptchuk, *The Web That Has No Weaver: Understanding Chinese Medicine* (New York: McGraw-Hill, 2000), 13.

21 Ibid, 8.

22 Sylvie Bérubé, *Dans le ventre d'Ève* (Paris: edition Vega, 2013), 209-217.

23 Ibid.

24 Joe Dispenza, *Becoming Supernatural: How Common People Are Doing the Uncommon* (New York: Hay House, Inc., 2017), 137.

25 Ibid, 103.

26 Yogi Bhajan, *The Aquarian Teacher: KRI International Kundalini Yoga Teacher Training Textbook Level 1 Instructor* (Kundalini Research Institute, 2003), 6.

Bibliography

Baron-Reid, Colette. *Uncharted: The Journey Through Uncertainty to Infinite Possibility*. New York: Hay House, Inc., 2016. Kindle.

Benson, Herbert. *The Relaxation Response*. New York: HarperTorch, 2000.

Bérubé, Sylvie. *Dans le ventre d'Ève*. Paris: edition Vega, 2013.

Bhajan, Yogi. *The Aquarian Teacher: KRI International Kundalini Yoga Teacher Training Textbook Level 1 Instructor*. Kundalini Research Institute, 2003.

Bolte Taylor, Jill. *My Stroke of Insight*. New York: Viking, Penguin Group, 2006. Kindle.

Campbell, Joseph. *The Hero with a Thousand Faces*. 3rd ed., Novato: New World Library, 2008.

Chevalier, Jean, and Alain Gheerbrant. *Dictionnaire des symboles : Mythes, rêves, coutumes, gestes, formes, figures, couleurs, nombres*. Paris : Robert Laffont S.A. and Jupiter, 1969.

Chödrön, Pema. *Comfortable with Uncertainty: 108 Teachings on Cultivating Fearlessness and Compassion*. Boston: Shambhala Publications, Inc., 2003.

———. *The Places That Scare You: A Guide to Fearlessness in Difficult Times*. Boston: Shambhala Publications, Inc., 2007.

———. *When Things Fall Apart: Heart Advice for Difficult Times*. Boston: Shambhala Publications, Inc., 2005.

Cumming, Heather, and Karen Leffler. *John of God: The Brazilian Healer Who's Touched the Lives of Millions*. New York and Hillsboro: Atria Books and Beyond Words, 2007. Kindle.

De La Rocheterie, Jacques. *La Symbologie des rêves : Le Corps humain.* Paris : Imago, 2012.

———. *La Symbologie des rêves : La nature.* Paris : Imago, 2012.

Dispenza, Joe. *Becoming Supernatural: How Common People Are Doing the Uncommon.* New York: Hay House, Inc., 2017.

———. *You Are the Placebo: Making Your Mind Matter.* New York: Hay House, Inc., 2014. Kindle.

———. *Breaking the Habit of Being Yourself: How to Lose Your Mind and Create a New One.* New York: Hay House, Inc., 2012. Kindle.

Dyer, Wayne W. *I Can See Clearly Now.* New York: Hay House, Inc., 2014. Kindle.

Dyer, Wayne W., and Esther Hicks (the teachings of Abraham). *Co-creating at Its Best: A Conversation Between Master Teachers (DVD).* New York: Hay House, Inc., 2014.

Hawkins, David R. *Healing and Recovery.* New York: Hay House, Inc., 2013. Kindle.

Hay, Louise. *You Can Heal Your Life.* New York: Hay House, Inc., 1984. Kindle.

Hay, Louise, Ahlea Khadro, and Heather Dane. *Loving Yourself to Great Health: Thoughts & Food—the Ultimate Diet.* New York: Hay House, Inc., 2014. Kindle.

Hesse, Herman. *Siddhartha.* New York: Bantam Books, 1971. Kindle.

Johnson, Robert A. *Inner Work: Using Dreams and Active Imagination for Personal Growth.* New York: HarperOne, 1989.

Kabat-Zinn, Jon. *Full Catastrophe Living: Using the Wisdom of Your Body and Mind to Face Stress, Pain, and Illness.* Revised and updated ed. New York: Bantam Books, 2013. Kindle.

Kaptchuk, Ted J. *The Web That Has No Weaver: Understanding Chinese Medicine.* New York: McGraw-Hill, 2000.

Katie, Byron. *Loving What Is: Four Questions That Can Change Your Life.* New York: Three Rivers Press, 2002.

Labonté, Marie Lise. *Au cœur de notre corps : Se libérer de nos cuirasses.* Montreal: Les éditions de l'Homme, 2000.

———. *Le déclic: Transformer la douleur qui détruit en douleur qui guérit.* Montreal: Les éditions de l'Homme, 2003.

Labonté, Marie Lise, and Nicolas Bornemisza. *Guérir grâce à nos images intérieures*. Montreal: Les éditions de l'Homme, 2006.

———. "Séminaire 'Se guérir grâce à ses images intérieures'". Produced by Productions Marie Lise Labonté. March 9, 2015. Video, 8 hours, 21 minutes. https://vimeo.com/121374415.

Moorjani, Anita. *Dying to Be Me: My Journey from Cancer, to Near Death, to True Healing*. New York: Hay House, Inc., 2012. Kindle.

Powers, Sarah. *Insight Yoga*. Boston: Shambala Publications, Inc., 2008.

Prabhavananda, Swami, and Christopher Isherwood. *How to Know God: The Yoga Aphorisms of Patanjali*. Hollywood: Vedanta Society, 1952.

Rankin, Lissa. *Mind Over Medicine: Scientific Proof That You Can Heal Yourself*. New York: Hay House, Inc., 2013. Kindle.

Ruiz, Don Miguel. *The Four Agreements: A Practical Guide to Personal Freedom*. San Rafael, California: Amber-Allen Publishing, Inc., 1997. Kindle.

The Sivananda Yoga Center. *The Sivananda Companion to Yoga*. New York: Fireside, 2000.

Schwartz, Robert. *Your Soul's Plan: Discovering the Real Meaning of the Life You Planned Before You Were Born*. Berkeley, California: Frog Books, 2007. Kindle.

Soulier, Olivier. *Sortir de la sclérose en plaques (DVD)*. Paris: edition Sens et Symboles, 2012.

Thackray, Gail. *Gail Thackray's Spiritual Journeys: Visiting John of God*. La Canadas, California: Indian Springs Publishing, 2012. Kindle.

Tolle, Eckhart. *A New Earth: Awakening to Your Life's Purpose*. New York: Plume, Penguin Group, 2006.

About the Author

Mounina was born in Montreal, Canada. At six months old, she moved to Mauritania, Africa, with her family, where she spent the first ten years of her life.

When she came back to Montreal, she followed the usual path. She went to school until she earned a bachelor's degree in mathematics from the University of Montreal. She was becoming an actuary and was working in pension plans. She became a kundalini yoga teacher.

In 2007 MS came to destroy the life as she knew it. She tried resisting and denying life for three years. She became a kripalu yoga teacher, as yoga is her passion.

Her disease became worse. She surrendered to life.

She found amazing mentors:
Marie Lise Labonté, with whom she became a holistic bodywork practitioner and experienced that body and mind are *one*.

Dr. Joe Dispenza, with whom she learned to change from the *inside out*. Mary Morrissey, with whom she became a transformational life coach, as transformation is her passion.

She realized that MS was gift *for* her because it led to her healing.

Her purpose is to share the healing power of love/life, to shift the perception around MS, and to help people empower themselves. To learn more, please visit her website: mouninabounaaly.com.